FLOGGING

BY *JOSEPH W. BEAN*

greenery press

Cover design by DesignTribe.

Published in the United States by Greenery Press. Distributed by SCB Distributors, Gardena, CA.

Readers should be aware that flogging, like all sexual activities, carries an inherent risk of physical and/or emotional injury. While we believe that following the guidelines set forth in this book will minimize that potential, the writers and publisher encourage you to be aware that you are taking some risk when you decide to engage in these activities, and to accept personal responsibility for that risk. In acting on the information in this book, you agree to accept that information as is and with all faults. Neither the authors, the publisher, nor anyone else associated with the creation or sale of this book is responsible for any damage sustained.

CONTENTS

THE TRUTH ABOUT *FLOGGING:* A FOREWORD

YOU CANNOT LEARN FLOGGING – TOP OR bottom – from a book. You will need real whips and, eventually, a real partner before you know flogging at all. Like every erotic activity, it's all in the sensations, and technique only matters when it is bad. Technique that is at all adequate, is adequate, and the sensations obliterate the difference between that and all the fancy moves and polished finesse of the best whip-handlers.

To imagine that you've learned flogging by reading this book would be like thinking you've found your way around Paris because you've closely examined a map of that city. The detailed map can tell you where the *boulangeries* are found, but it can not give you the heady sense of having smelled the *baguettes* coming out of the oven; it can tell you how to locate *Place de la Concorde*, but even with your finger right on the spot, you will not feel the awe and fear that are sure to overcome you the first time you stand on the curb and contemplate crossing the traffic circle in any direction.

So, why read a book about flogging if you're not going to learn everything from it? For the same reason you'd be smart to look at a map before setting out to enjoy Paris. The more you know before you set out on your journey, the faster you'll find your way, and the more of the "good stuff" you'll get to on each trip. Even if you've been doing flogging for years, it can't hurt to know how someone else does it... and, why not me?

The truth about *Flogging* is that I have had a great time writing it, and I think you'll have a great time reading it. I learned a lot about how I approach and do my favorite scene by organizing the information for you in this book, and I believe – whether you are a novice or an old hand with whips – you are sure to learn something from it too.

There are, of course, many people to be thanked for various kinds of help when any book is written. In this case, the people who deserve the most gratitude are the leathermen and leatherwomen who have flogged me – as often teaching me what not to do as what to do – and the ones who have bared their bodies and trusted me to come at them with whips in hand.

I am also grateful to Tony DeBlase who read the earliest drafts of the first parts of this book and made, as was his habit, few remarks, but every one of them insightful and useful. (Tony was the most important influence on the Topping side of my flogging life, probably not much aware of it himself.) Chuck Renslow has patiently allowed me to divert time that should have been spent on other projects into the writing of this book, and the book could not have been written without that accommodation. Bill Stadt has meant more to me during these months than he will ever understand, bearing my grumbling and letting me complain until I had nothing left to complain about. His attention and love actually make my sometimes out-of-control life seem meaningful, in fact. So, it is with love and appreciation to one of the leather world's truly under-appreciated heroes that …

I DEDICATE THIS BOOK TO BILL STADT.

A FEW WORDS ABOUT WORDS IN *FLOGGING*

BEING A MAN WHO USUALLY PLAYS WITH other men and always identifies himself as gay, I am more acutely aware than some others might be of the "pronoun problem." It is always with me. I have settled the question of he/she and his/her in this book the easy way. That is, I have typed male or female pronouns indiscriminately when the sex of the individual referred to is not relevant. I have also tried to be consistent so that no one seems to get a linguistic sex-change in mid-paragraph.

In laying out the scenes in the book, I chose to have one fem-dom, one male-dom, one male-male and one female-female scene. As there were four scenes in the outline, this seemed to be a complete and entirely acceptable answer. But it is not, of course. Who would get the scene that "went wrong" or the one that "got heavy" or the one with no flogging in it or the one with all the novice materials? Who indeed? I promise, cross my heart, that no planning at all with regard to sex or orientation went into these choices. For instance, male-dom, heterosexual players must not think the fact that the basic lessons are taught in examining "their" scene means I figure they need "novice-level" help. Nor should lesbians suppose that I believe they are more likely to have a scene go badly.

I suppose I could be more sensitive about references to sex and sexual orientation. I could have counted the number of male and female, het and gay references and edited them into perfect balance, but then I'd be left trying to figure out what perfect balance is. Fifty-fifty both times? Try to match the percentages in the world population? What? So, I have permitted accident to rule all. There is no need to blame me for thinking up my choices because I thought not at all about them.

Being a person who thinks it more important to handle a whip well than to be able to describe its parts in historically accurate terminology, and a person who believes flogging well matters more than being able to name the instruments used in the flogging, I have used the word "whip" very loosely throughout this book. It does not specifically mean a single-tailed whip. In fact, here, it means nothing of the kind unless the context proves that it does. "Whip" and "instrument" are the generics in this book, encompassing floggers both flat and braided, cats regardless of the number of tails they may have, and all the variants we see in the leather stores and dungeons all the time. In fact, I have avoided using too many names either for the parts of whips or for their styles and configurations. This seemed the only wise course of action since, as I have been traveling around the country for many years talking to and with leatherfolk, I have come to the conclusion that what is a cat one place is a flogger elsewhere, what is a flog to one man is a flog*ger* to the next, what are the tails of a "whip" in one situation will be called the ends in another. Whip makers disagree as much as whip users about some of the terminology, and when we speak of quirts or stock whips or sjamboks, the arguments can get heated. The words are usually not needed and certainly contribute little or nothing to the success of a scene. So, they have usually been ignored here. Or, when specific terms are used, I have tried to be clear about what I mean by the word. Disagree if you will, but don't bother to argue with me or anyone about what kind of elbow it takes to make a whip a *stock* whip and whether it can have more than one tail or whether a quirt can have more than two. Those of us most eager to use whips and have them used on us are not likely to argue back. We'll wander off, instead, in search of someone looking for a scene instead of an argument.

Nonetheless, to keep things simple, I have added boxed texts throughout the book with illustrations by Chris M. and basic "definitions" of the items discussed. If they help, use them. If not, just enjoy the excellent drawings and read on.

FLOGGING: AN INTRODUCTION TO SYMPHONIC SEXUAL ECSTASY

Flogging is a passion for me. I like a lot of things, many of them are ways to do SM or have sex, but only flogging – doing the flogging, that is, swinging the whips myself – is really a passion. I might even say at this point that I need to flog. Nothing else clears my mind and refreshes my heart as flogging does, and no other form of exercise gets me so high. I admit that part of the "trip" for me is in the dominance, the control, even the power play, but there is so much more to it. I really want to share that with as many people as I can, literally! And this book is an opportunity to share my passion in another way.

I am assuming that you wouldn't have picked up this book if you didn't have some interest in flogging, but I am not assuming that you know what flogging really is. In untrained fantasy, it may be nothing more than a form or submission or dominance, or a way that a person gets turned on for what they think of as "real sex" to follow. In any case, in fantasy, being flogged never really hurts and the scene never turns out badly.

Flogging might seem to be many things depending on fictions and fantasies and rumors, and depending on experience. Yes, flogging involves one person repeatedly striking another with a whip of one sort or another. Yes, it is a beating from one point of view, and it is really sex for some people. The dictionary definition of flogging surprisingly doesn't require whips at all. A single lash, a belt, a rod or cane… just about anything that comes to hand and is used to beat another person qualifies for Webster and his friends. The etymologists tend to think of flogging as a punishment, but flogging is also sensual massage and love-making and access to ecstasy for some. In Finland, where the national pastime is the sauna, friends flog one another as part of the steam-bath experience. In the Arab and Moslem nations and in much of the Asian Pacific, people are flogged for minor infractions of the law. The range is very broad, but this book is very specific: Here, flogging is meant to please both parties, meant to be something they look forward to, consent to, enjoy, and repeat.

For me, as a Top (meaning, as I said, I am the one on the handle end of the whip these days), first and foremost, a flogging is a dance, an artistic cooperation with another person.

To take that musical analogy a few steps further would not be pointless. Think of the possible styles in which music can be composed. From a classical symphony with a number of movements at varying tempos and in varying moods to hot jazz with surprising improvisations and repetitions, from ballad-like storytelling to wildly romantic torch songs. The list goes on endlessly from there, and any of these musical styles would be a good model for understanding *some* flogging scene, although it is unlikely that you would often want to think of a musical style and actually use that style (or composition) as a basis for building your scene. And rhythm is essential in music as it is in flogging. In music, as in flogging, variations in rhythm create interest and give the work vitality. Finally, every scene, like every musical composition, requires an end that is intended and controlled in some sense. The finale can be a screeching halt sometimes as it often is with early modernist music, or it can fully resolve all the previous "musical statements" in the piece in the way the romantic-period classics do.

There is no one way to do a flogging, no one way to feel about the activity of flogging, but there is one truth about flogging that is immutable: The result is pleasure, even joy for both parties. This is another musical analogy. The composer is gratified when the music he creates is well received. The listener is satisfied when the music she hears touches her deeply and with positive effects.

Mostly, floggings are as private as sex, but sometimes they happen in other settings. People sometimes do flogging scenes at play parties, events scheduled by clubs or groups to provide safe and accommodating conditions for SM. When flogging is done in this semi-public way – and it is at every play party – it becomes an opportunity for you and me and everyone present to learn about flogging by watching and, in a very real way, to participate just by being present. The energy around a flogging that is working well can not be contained. It touches everyone in reach and offers them a taste of its joyful results.

Fortunately, there are clubs and organizations all over the world that help newcomers to SM find their place in the interpenetrating communities and fetish circles and networks of known practitioners. Without these clubs, how would we find each other? Well, people have been doing it for millennia. Ancient Greek art shows floggings in progress more than 2,400 years ago, but I'm glad to live in an era that gives us easy options – never as easy as we imagine they should be – for meeting appropriate partners for our tastes, including flogging.

But the truth that matters about flogging is always smaller and far more intimate than any of the ancient history or the modern clubs or even the personal fantasies. What matters is that two people meet, match and turn towards the unknown together, ready to help each other into the emotional stratosphere or beyond.

It is my hope, above and beyond everything else, that you – every reader – will discover that you really can touch or be touched, fly or be flown, love and be loved through flogging.

In the chapters that follow, you and I are voyeurs. We will look in on some flogging scenes and discuss them. We will mercilessly hold our fantasies up to the lighted reality of these scenes and risk whatever changes that may entail. I obviously risk much less than you do. I have been there, and I chose and composed the players and the scenes in this book. As an unquestioning bottom for almost 19 years, I know what is possible for the person catching the blows of a whip – both those well aimed and lovingly delivered and the other kinds. As a Top for 18 years since then, I know what magic and sexual wonder is possible from this side of the whip as well. But honesty is always a risk, so I mean it when I say, "Let's go. Let's take together whatever we have coming."

SCENE ONE

LEILA AND JIM AT AN SM CLUB PARTY

JIM IS A MASTER, WELL KNOWN IN THE local community, with a reputation for doing good work with floggers and whips. Joanne, another respected Top, once introduced Jim at a cocktail party as "the high priest of flogging." He took the compliment in stride and met it with no false modesty. He's good, and he knows it. In fact, he doesn't know anyone better, except the man who taught him. Jim is in his late forties, tall, trim and groomed to have a somewhat mischievously evil appearance that feels completely appropriate on him. He always moves through parties at The Club dressed in tight leather pants and tall, shiny boots. He wears no shirt, and everyone seems to think of the baring of his torso as a plus for the party decor. He also happens to be especially attractive to Leila, a submissive who thinks of herself as quite a catch but, until now, perhaps not experienced enough to be able to please a heavy player like Jim.

Leila has been attending the parties of The Club for several months, and has taken every opportunity to watch Jim's scenes. He works fast and hits hard. The women he flogs are always thrilled with the scenes, but they are also the most experienced – seldom the most attractive – women in The Club. Leila knows that Jim has sometimes watched her scenes too. More than once, she has noticed him just turning to leave as her blindfold is removed. She is 30-something, built a little heavier than a fashion model, but undoubtedly well-proportioned. She is particularly pleased with what she sees in the full-length mirror when she turns her back to the mirror and looks over her shoulder. Her back is smooth and tapers from gently rounded shoulders to a waist that looks much smaller than the 32 inches it actually measures. Her long, dark blond hair lies in soft, natural waves over her upper spine, gathered, as it always is, in a loose, low-tied pony tail which she can easily switch to hang across her shoulder when she wants her back bare.

Finally, at the "Bottoms Up" theme party – a sort of Sadie Hawkins affair at which submissives are expected to approach dominants – Leila got up the nerve to ask Jim to for a flogging scene. "Sir," she began, more than a little nervously, "pardon me, but I was hoping that you might like to...."

When Leila's voice caught in her throat, Jim took over. "Let's talk," he said, "come over here." He led her to a bench where, without saying another word, he began to lay out his whips. It was an impressive collection for one person to bring to a party, more than a dozen instruments, every one of them very different from the others. After the whips were lined up on the bench, Jim took Leila's hand – touching her for the first time ever – and moved her around so she was standing directly in front of the whip display. He then stepped behind her.

Jim whispered into Leila's hair, "You look at the whips while I look at you... at your back. You don't mind if I touch?"

"Touch all you want," Leila answered.

"And in any area?"

"You know the rules of The Club," Leila stated, just slightly defensively.

"Yes," Jim answered. "No penetration of any orifice with any body part, not even a finger. I understand that. I just get... sometimes, I get affectionate, you know."

"I know. It's one of the things I like about the way you work. Flogging is really SM sex the way you do it. It's something I am counting on. If this," she said, indicating the array of whips with a sweeping gesture, "is going to work for me, I think you will have to… well, you may find it useful to, er, touch me, the way I've seen you do with others."

"Useful? Maybe. Pleasant for both of us anyway, I'd hope." With that, Jim put his hands on Leila's sides, allowing them to slide slowly down, his thumbs pressing more than gently into her back as they moved, till his open hands rested on her beautifully flaring, generously rounded hips. She could feel his breath on the top of her head, then on the side of her face.

"I always use The Club's safewords, but hope I'll never hear them, by the way. I never do a flogging without the first two whips on the left," Jim said, "and I really like it when I get to use the one at the far right, but that's not very often. Look them over. Touch them, pick them up. Think about it. If you have questions, ask. Then, when you are ready, I want you to answer two questions. First, which whips would you like to 'taste' tonight? And, second, which of my tools would you most like not to become acquainted with right away?" Jim was more accustomed to asking only the second question. The answer could be very revealing. Tonight, however, it was "Bottoms Up," and he was trying to stay in the spirit of the thing.

Leila didn't want to move out of Jim's gentle grip, but she was determined to do what he had asked. She placed her hands on his and moved half a step closer to the bench. As she hoped, he moved in with her. When she bent to caress the tail of a flogger, he pressed forward just a bit, following her butt with his groin, letting her feel the heat and hardness of his leather-covered crotch against the naked coolness of her ass-cheek. She spent only a minute or two looking at the whips before she turned toward Jim.

As Leila turned, Jim encircled her with his arms, not pressing her to his body, but keeping her very close. "Yes," he said, drawing the word out seductively.

"Sir," Leila answered, now feeling more confident and at ease, "I'd like you to use whatever whips you like, but I will answer your questions, of course. Because I am worried that I will not be able to take the kind of heavy whipping you sometimes give, I would like a long warm-up… slow… starting easy, to get me as ready as possible. You know, I want to go as far as I can with this. And, that makes me think that we should include another of your soft, easy whips in the beginning. So, can we add the horsehair whip to the ones that 'must' be used?"

She stopped and looked at Jim, feeling submission take hold in her emotions. Jim just nodded, then asked, "Is there something else?"

"Well, if you don't mind, one of these heavy floggers would probably be easy for me to take. I know that when I am just playing around – even with myself – the heavy ones feel good pretty quickly. They don't… well, you know, they don't cause a lot of pain-pain, if you know what I mean."

"They don't sting that much," Jim said, showing he knew exactly what she meant. "I will use that one," he said, pointing to a broad-tailed, fifty-strand buffalo flogger, but Leila didn't turn to look. He continued, "I will keep in mind what you are saying. And, before we begin, I need to know a few more things about you. Of course, I know who you are and who your friends are, I know what kind of pain scenes you usually get involved with and what I have never seen you do. But I need to know about your body and its limitations. Do you wear lenses or take medications? Do you mark easily or not, and do you mind being marked? Do you bleed easily and will it end the scene for you if you bleed?"

"I think," Leila answered with great care, "that there is no medical information I need to give you. The only medication I take is a birth control pill, and I don't wear lenses to these parties. That means I can not see plainly at a great distance, but I don't need to, do I?"

"And?" Jim questioned again.

"And I am single and living alone, so I don't mind marks. I have never bled in a scene and don't especially turn on the to the idea."

"But, for me?"

"For you, Sir, I would be pleased to go as far as you can take me. Maybe I will bleed. I am a little worried about that, but only a little. Do you understand?"

"I do," Jim whispered. Then, wrapping his arms around Leila again, holding her very close, he kissed her forehead and whispered. "Take a moment to think of submitting to me, to consider that you are likely to explore territory in yourself that is not very familiar to you, that you are going to trust me to launch you into yourself and that I am going to trust you to bring me along as far as you can on that journey. Take a moment to be sure you are ready and free and able to put yourself in my hands without reservations. Then join me at that cross over there." Jim nodded in the direction of a Saint Andrew's cross on the wall.

"What if that cross is not available in a few minutes?" Leila asked.

"I am not asking you to wonder about that, my dear, just meet me there when you are ready to begin."

"Yes, Sir," Leila whispered, "I'll be there shortly."

In the next few minutes, Leila wandered around, feeling herself letting go and giving in to the control Jim wanted to have. She questioned herself again about the wisdom of asking for a flogging from such an experienced player, a person who often beat women very long and so hard. But, yes, she was definitely ready for that… in her mind. Would her body cooperate? That's where the trust came in, she understood. That's where Jim's experience would matter most.

For some reason, Leila felt a need to go to the bathroom where there was a full-length mirror. She looked herself over, giving special attention to as much of her own back as she was able to see. Suddenly, she was very eager to see it again, marked with the work of Master Jim. She was as ready as she would ever be.

She went to the Saint Andrew's cross, where she found Jim. He had moved the bench over near the cross and had rearranged the whips according to their discussion. The horsehair whip and the two whips he "always" used were at one end of the arrangement. The heavy flogger Leila had liked was next. Then there was another heavy flogger with very broad, almost belt-like tails, and another with flat braided tails. And, at the end, a braided cat with thin tails ending in hard knots, the one Jim had said he always liked to get to. And there was a short single tailed whip, which Leila believed qualified to be called a signal whip, coiled loosely on the end of the bench. Jim's canvas duffel bag was on the floor open; Leila chose to spend no time looking into that mysterious space.

Leila moved in close to Jim, but he nodded toward the cross as she approached. She turned to the cross, and in giving up her hoped-for caress, she felt a thrill of sexual submission tingle in her crotch and spread across her ass cheeks and onto her back. She encouraged the sensation and felt its warmth prickle up her spine, almost itching as it moved. She put her hands up on the cross, but Jim moved them down. He had attached a pair of fur-lined restraints to the center point on the back of the cross. It took only a moment for him to buckle the restraints around her wrists. Then, with practiced ease, he slid her feet apart, stopping with each of her boots well inside the spread legs of the cross. His last touch was on her shoulder as he pushed her ponytail around her neck to hang, out of harm's way, in front of her.

Jim pressed in close behind Leila, dangling the horsehair whip so that its spiky tips brushed her ass and lower back as he smoothed his empty hand over her upper back. His warm palm and strong fingers pressed and pulled at every inch of Leila's upper back, his fingertips marking the edges of the strike zone with added pressure. The sensual touch was not exactly what Leila had prepared for, but she appreciated the moment to connect with Jim and clarify her resolve again.

Then, without warning, Jim stepped back and began brushing Leila's back with the horsehair. The first strokes were a little scratchy and not really all that pleasant, but they were the message she needed to get: The flogging has begun. For a moment, Leila may have doubted her commitment to this scene with its potential to be harder and heavier than any flogging she had been given before, but… well, it was Jim… Master Jim.

As the strokes with the horsehair came faster, they also grew harder. Some strokes – the ones for which Jim pulled back till only the tips of the coarse hair raced across her back – felt like a flock of razor blades flying across her skin, too sharp and too fast to really hurt, but not the gentle warming that she expected from the horsehair either.

Soon, Leila's mind was entirely absorbed with just two things, the warmth gathering and spreading in her back and the fact that she was finally giving herself to Jim. Meantime, Jim was thinking how beautiful Leila was, how superbly she displayed her submission, how the impulses to be gentle and to tear into her back with all his strength struggled in his muscles. He knew he would have plenty of opportunity to be gentle, to soothe and caress and warm Leila's back, and he had a growing clarity about the developing opportunity to exercise the other impulses as well.

After several minutes of increasingly heavy strokes with the horsehair, sometimes letting up to soft, cushiony pressure, but building overall to more and more heavily landed strokes, Jim stopped. He let his body weight drop against Leila's back, then slid one hand up between her body and his own. The sweat on his chest made him stick to Leila a little, but his hand pressed in, deeply massaging Leila's back muscles as he breathed on her ear and nibbled at her shoulder. A moment later, he pushed himself away from the unresisting body, allowing a degree of rougher, more dominant strength to come through in the way he raised himself off her.

Then, without a moment's hesitation, Jim slapped Leila's back with the light, flat-tailed leather flogger. He had somehow switched tools with one hand while caressing her back with the other. That first leather stroke bit into Leila's back, and she had to wrestle a little with an impulse to shout out… perhaps even to complain of the surprise. Instead, she involuntarily swung her head back, bent her shoulders back, leaned back at the waist as much as the restraints permitted, and heaved out a low, murmuring breath. Then, slowly composing herself, she eased herself back onto the cross and repeatedly drew her shoulders forward, effectively stretching the hot, red skin of her back, opening herself for more of whatever Jim had in mind. She felt her hair touching her back and gave her head a tightly controlled shake. Jim had already noticed. He reached in and lightly tossed the ponytail over Leila's shoulder again.

For quite a long time after that, the leather flogger landed on one half of her upper back and then the other. The strokes made contact from up near her shoulders and slid a few inches down her back. They landed with increasing weight over the course of many minutes, then they changed. First the direction of the whip's movement was adjusted, then the way the "heavy" tails landed. If they were hitting high and sliding before, now they seemed to strike with many inches of the gathered tails falling together on her skin, more pressing than hitting her. Then, almost imperceptibly, the rhythm changed: several strokes would brush by, not touching Leila's back at all, but pushing a cool wind across from very close. After two or three such close passes, the flogger tails would land across her back, all the tails falling together into her muscles, hitting both sides of her back at the same time with a deep thud then dragging slightly downward and sliding across her skin till they were free for more close passes and then more broad, heavy strokes.

Leila hardly noticed when Jim changed from the light leather flogger to the heavier one. In fact, it felt as though he might have been switching back and forth between the two for some time when she became aware of the husky, forced-out breaths with which Jim accompanied each stroke of the heavy flogger. He was really working, and Leila liked that he was having to work… that she was handling his flogging well enough for that. Actually, she was handling nothing; she was enjoying all of it. It had not been a problem at all to rise to the level of Jim's flogging. She found herself signaling with her postures and the slight sounds she made that she wanted more and more. And it was true, she did.

Again, Jim was pressing his sweat-wet body on Leila's back, and both of his hands were rubbing and digging at her back, carrying the warmth of the flogging over her skin with them. She felt a whip handle between their bodies sometimes and realized he had the whip hanging around his own neck.

Jim smoothed the heat radiating from Leila's back, out and away, over her ass cheeks, across her ribs and up the front of her body. He cupped her breasts in his hands, then pushed forward with his whole body, forcing her breasts into his hands, his wrists and forearms resting on the uprights of the cross. Using his upper arms and the weight of his chest, Jim forced Leila's body to move in a tight circle: lifting, left, lowering, right, over and over, her hard, swollen nipples tracing tiny circles in each of Jim's lightly cupped hands. His right leg slid forcefully between her legs, lifting her slightly and rubbing in and out. For a second, Leila thought the flogging must be over, but the approach of an orgasm prevented her from considering the thought very clearly.

As Leila reached the peak of her ecstasy, Jim pulled his hands away and lifted off of her body. He started lightly slapping her back with his open hands. Sometimes he slapped several times in rapid succession, sometimes he slapped her hot back then rubbed away the sting of the impact before lifting his hand from her pain-hungry skin to slap again.

Leila was moaning loudly, on the brink of screaming really, when Jim stepped back further and started softly whipping her with another heavy instrument. The soft strokes of this whip, with the weight of its gathered tails, were heavier than any of the previous whips could have been. She barely noticed the new whip though, and cared not at all what it was. The sensations were exciting, and she was not concerned at this point how Jim was creating them. In fact, Jim was now using his favorite whip, a flat-braided leather flogger – some people would call it a cat-o-nine tails, even though the tails ended in leaf-shaped tags of leather rather than the traditional knots expected on a cat. The whip landed with thudding authority every time, mostly in the heavy strokes that stretched across Leila's back from side to side, coming now from the right, now from the left.

There was no way for Leila to know when or why she had started shouting out as each stroke landed. She was barely aware of the sounds escaping her throat, and didn't care anyway. Then the pleasured shouts and moans suddenly grew sharper – now sounding almost frightened – as the strokes became sharper and more penetrating. Jim didn't stop whipping her, but the strokes changed to the familiar top-to-lower back kind, each shot landing lightly at Leila's shoulders and sliding down her back in a right and left rhythm too complex to be understood or anticipated, but also unmistakably measured and controlled. The whip, seemingly working on its own, continued to torment Leila's back as Jim moved around to look at her face and kiss her cheek. "Just a little longer," he said, adding a whispered "please."

Leila's answer was perfectly clear, even if Jim couldn't exactly hear the words. Yes, she could go on, but the phrase "a little longer" was welcome, perhaps very welcome.

"Want to count?" Jim whispered.

"Ahng," Leila said, meaning, "Yes, Sir, thank you, Sir."

"OK. We'll do six more," Jim said. "That's six good ones, only count the good ones, and count loud. Got it?"

"Ahng," Leila agreed.

Jim stepped back a threw the whip against Leila's back harder than any shot up to that moment.

"One, Sir!" Leila shouted very clearly. Then she took a moment to arrange herself and spread her back, signaling that she was ready for number two.

Three or four more heavy strokes landed squarely on Leila's back, the last one being both out of rhythm and much heavier, before she shouted out, "Two, Sir."

There might have been six successful strokes after that before Leila counted, "Three, Sir." And, there must have been twenty more before she finally had to say, "Six, Sir, thank you, Sir." At that, she began to cry and tremble uncontrollably.

Jim held her tight, kissed her neck and the side of her face repeatedly, then lifted her away from the cross. She didn't even notice when he unbuckled her restraints. Leila rested against Jim's chest, her hands moving uncontrollably, both trying to dig into the sweaty chest and to close the gap between the sides of her face and hard, hairy skin on which she continued to cry for a minute or two.

Eventually, Jim turned her around to face away from himself. Supporting her with his left arm extended across her ribs just below her breasts, he lightly touched a few spots on her back, ran his hand even more lightly over the hot, flogged skin and asked quietly, "You OK?"

Leila just nodded. She was so much more than OK, but she was in no state to explain it. Anyway, she was sure Jim knew exactly where and how she was. Yes, exactly… all of it.

After a few more minutes of kisses and comforting touch, Jim stood Leila upright, holding her just long enough to be sure she knew was no longer supported by his arm, and stepped back to arm's length. "You're not bleeding at all. You could just leave it to dry, or I could have my slave-girl wash it up for you. You want that?"

Leila shook her head. Soon, she would go home. There she would shower… yes, a long, warm shower. She would let the water run over her back for a very long time, probably reliving the sweet sensations of the flogging in a way that was familiar to her. Then she would slip into a cotton T-shirt to sleep, and she knew she would have sweet dreams, very sweet dreams tonight.

The next day, Jim called Leila to ask if she was still OK about the scene. She was. He also hinted that he'd like to do it again, and she said very plainly that she would be looking forward to the next time.

"Great," Jim said to himself as he hung up the phone. He had been wanting Leila for a long time, and next time, he would not be letting her go home alone, keeping the afterglow of the flogging to herself.

Scene One Examined

The Basics of Flogging

Flogging is a relatively easy SM technique to learn, and one of the few that can probably be learned safely by experimentation. The learning curve can be much faster, of course, if you have information and instruction. There is a great deal of both in the scene we have just witnessed. It should, however, be understood that flogging is also one of the ways of doing SM that becomes extremely different for different people in different situations at different times. As we "watch" other scenes later in this book, you will see that.

Jim and Leila are good models for us to look at as we consider the basics of flogging. They are both experienced players – although at different levels of experience – and they are doing their scene under the controlled and presumably monitored circumstances of a party. There are a few other things about their interaction in the period before the scene that we should look at.

No matter what kind of SM scene you want to undertake, the proper precursors are the same: networking and negotiation. Networking gets you the right partner; negotiating gets you the right scene.

GETTING THE RIGHT PARTNER

Networking means taking the time to find a person who is considered safe and trustworthy by checking with friends and scene-buddies. In the case of a club contact, the networking is easy, but it should not be ignored. There are two reasons to still give your attention to the effort to network effectively, even when the partner you are considering is a regular at a club or munch or in some circle of friends you know. First, some people in clubs are tolerated, but not really trusted. They may even be on some kind of probation as members or invitees of the club. This is information you should have and seriously consider. And, second, not everyone at every party is appropriate for every other person to do scenes with. Maybe the person you are looking at with longing is not a completely honest negotiator. He might be very good at the scenes he does, and be accepted by others only because they already know the difference between what he promises and what he delivers. Or, perhaps, she is not so much good as showy. Sometimes a scene that is more show than controlled stimulation is OK. Other times, it is just too far from what you want to be worth the effort.

You may also get a good deal of interesting and even surprising information about yourself in the process of networking to find a partner. If people say things like, "Oh, I think she's too serious for you," or "that won't work because he plays really hard," you know that you are perceived as a lighter or less serious player. Like it or not, you learn. Of course, you are the one who has to weigh the information you collect about yourself and the partners you are considering. So, you can choose to change the perception of yourself by acting otherwise than as expected. Nonetheless, you should not just get upset about the information you collect if it disagrees with your perception of yourself. It could be true. There may be a difference between the way you imagine yourself and the way you live and play. At least consider the possibility that others who watch you do actually know what they're seeing.

Getting the facts about a potential partner must go no further than that – getting the facts. There could be all kinds of facts that you should have, and you should have whatever information you can get before agreeing to a scene with anyone. There is obviously a risk of becoming so informed that the mystery or sexy tinge of danger are networked out of the scene, but that's a risk worth taking in most cases. It is also a risk that is easily avoided by going only as far in the networking as necessary. Going too far can reduce networking to gossiping anyway. On the other hand, not going far enough can mean failing to collect information required for your safety and satisfaction.

What you want is a partner who is safe – will take no for an answer when necessary, for instance – but one who also does scenes like the ones you are looking for. An experienced and even expert master of single-tail whips is not necessarily a great flogging Top.

So, step one in the direction of any scene with any partner is to tap your network to find or check on a partner. What you want to know is whether the persons you're looking at (or for) – particularly if they are Tops, Masters/Mistresses, Dominants – can be trusted to play safely, to take no for an answer even after the scene begins, to do the kind of scene you want at a level that is within your range.

In the course of networking, you will very likely get conflicting opinions and gratuitous information. File everything away and remember that the final choice to go forward with a particular potential partner is your own. You cannot blame others, later, for not advising you strongly enough one way or the other. All SM is actually an at-your-own-risk activity, networking and dungeon masters notwithstanding.

Stopping when you have the facts not only prevents unwarranted gossiping, it also keeps the potential partner mysterious enough to be sexy. If the networking doesn't turn you away from your intention to play with someone, the next step in the direction of the scene is negotiation. This can be as much or little conversation as necessary. Sometimes, it can be no more than a few words exchanged between partners who are relatively familiar with each other or are playing under circumstances that are sufficiently controlled by rules and monitors. When you have played with someone before, the negotiating can sometimes be reduced to a few silent glances that merely confirm that both parties are sober enough, interested at the moment, and in a mood to go ahead. Still, jumping to the conclusion that negotiating is not needed can be a big problem.

GETTING THE RIGHT SCENE

What negotiation should cover – either in words or accumulated information – is everything on the list below. Much or most of it can be managed without discussion. For many people, the sexual component of the scene or the psychology of dominance and submission will require that the overt portions of the negotiating be done at another time and place, days or weeks before the actual scene. This protects the atmosphere of the scene without denying either player the protection of having negotiated his or her own safety. It also gives both people time to reconsider.

Negotiate or know/communicate all of the following:

Safewords or signals should be understood or their absence mutually accepted. There are often default safewords these days at club-sponsored events. Red for "stop," yellow for "let up" or "check for a problem," and green for "more" are common, but anything is possible. Most people find that a safeword that says all is well or that the bottom wants more is not much used. Others are disturbed by the out-of-scene-dynamic feel of words like red, yellow and green. Still others want their safewords to be as far out of the working dynamic as possible.

For some people, the atmosphere around a flogging can be rather delicate, and safewords have to be very carefully selected for their scenes. If a Top requires a bottom to give a seamless show of submission, in fact, the very concept of a safeword could become problematic. (Some bottoms are just as sensitive in this way.) Since safewords are signals given by the bottom and meant to alter or stop a scene, it is just impossible for some players to introduce this "reversal of the dynamics of SM" into a scene. There are a few relatively simple solutions that retain the most important features of the safeword system while avoiding the possible problem.

First, a couple undertaking a flogging can take every precaution with the bondage they are to use and make every effort to understand each other in advance. The Top can assume full responsibility for the result of a scene without the protection of safewords. Then, maybe they can agree on just one safeword – a total deal-breaker, something simple like "safeword" shouted by the bottom only in the event that the scene must stop immediately. After all, if it comes to this, there is no need to try to defend the scene atmosphere anyway. This is not

Safewords generally work well with flogging – a single word can stop a scene immediately. However, with toys like clamps, which hurt more coming off than staying on, a safeword may be too little, too late.

the safest option. It is not something you can be advised to choose, but it's better than ignoring the issue or claiming to be playing with no safewords. In point of fact, this is a sort of default system that is in effect, agreed upon or not, in every SM interaction.

Second, the Top can give the bottom safewords or safeword-substitutes that are not dangerous to the SM atmosphere. One possibility is to have the bottom speak directly to the Top if there is a problem that can be solved, and perhaps speak to the bottom using the Top's actual name, which he or she would be forbidden to use at any other time. If words are a problem, other signals can be agreed on, well within the demands of the aura created for the scene.

There is another way to go that many people don't like for one reason or another. Still, something that works nicely with relaxed partners is that they just agree that the bottom (and Top) may say what they feel they need to say at any moment. In this case, they are playing without safewords, but not without the safety net provided by the conventional safewords. Instead of "yellow," the bottom would be able to say, "that restraint is beginning to hurt my wrist." This kind of communication would wreck the scene for some players, but a clever bottom can say what is needed with sufficient attention to respect and scene-supportive behavior.

It is a matter of some importance to have the safeword/verbal feedback set-up (or its absence) acceptable and comfortable for both parties before the scene is underway. And, it should be noticed that different people may have very different ideas of when the scene has begun.

Sexy conversation may be "just" negotiation to one person, but an integral part of the scene to another. A little sensitivity to your partner's mood will probably make this clear. Sometimes either signals or spotters are used. Signals such as stomping or dropping a clasped item can be used when the bottom is gagged or otherwise unable to speak effectively. A spotter – someone who is familiar with the bottom and is commissioned to watch the scene and speak for the bottom – can be a big turn-on and a useful participant in the scene, or a turn-off and scene destroyer. The difference is who, with whom, under what circumstances and all that. Personal preference, in the end, is everything.

Medical limitations and facts, such as drugs you may be taking or whether you are wearing or should be wearing lenses, should be discussed before play. Some drugs can change the way you perceive and respond to stimulation. In some cases, a flogging Top may prefer not to flog a bottom who is taking mood-altering or pain-reducing drugs, for example. Lenses or limited eyesight can matter. A person wearing lenses would, for instance, usually be well advised to remove the lenses before being hooded or blindfolded. In other cases, the Top might choose a different blindfold – one that places no pressure at all on the eyes – if playing with a lens-wearing bottom. Weak or arthritic joints might need to be mentioned, and there can be any number of other medical facts of potential interest. If you are too new to flogging to know what may be important, offer more rather than less information.

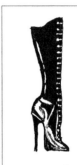

For many players, prolonged standing in high heels would be a medical limitation.

Generally speaking, it is not hard to think what medical information you might want to reveal before starting a flogging scene, but maybe a few additional examples will help. If you have high blood pressure and complications from that condition or any form of heart disease, it could matter when you reach a certain level of excitement or stimulation. Arthritic joints or carpal tunnel syndrome could be good reasons to use special precautions with regard to bondage or to consider playing without bondage. A bad back could need special attention. Obviously, any problem for which you carry emergency medication should be mentioned, and you should see that the person you are playing with (and perhaps others nearby) are aware of where your medication is. (In plain view in the play space would be easy.) If your blood is not able to clot normally because of disease or prescription drugs, you will probably want to avoid the risk of cuts or other causes of bleeding in the scene.

If there is anything about revealing medical information that is surprising to inexperienced players, it is that this is hardly less important for Tops than for bottoms. A Top in sudden need of medication is every bit as important as a bottom with the same need.

Limits of pain-tolerance and your expectations about how you will react to the stimulation that is being considered might be among the things you'll want to communicate. You don't really know with absolute certainty before a scene what your limits are. They can contract for the simplest and smallest of reasons (a cold breeze in the room or the sound of a neighboring scene), and they can expand in the most surprising way under the ministrations of an appropriately seductive Top. Still, you may want to give whatever indications you can of your limits. This was done in Jim and Leila's scene when they were considering which floggers to use. And, if you know something of how you are likely react to a flogging, you might want to tell the dominant what you know, particularly if you suspect your responses could be misinterpreted. For instance, if you know you are likely to start crying or to shout out, "No, I can't take this," when you are thrilled to continue taking all of it and more, say so in advance. Some people will also respond with anger when flogged, but not mean to have that taken personally or used as any excuse to slow down or stop the flogging. Others will curse or make no sound or become physically tense. If, in a few words, you can communicate what the person wielding the whip can expect along these lines, you will give your Top a much more proficient understanding of your scene "language."

Scene-stopping words and attitudes should be explained. If there are words you thrive on or can not abide or attitudes you warm up to and others that repel you, tell your partner about them. Again, no great introspective discussion is called for. Just a sentence, for example, can tell the Top that you do or don't like to be called "boy" or that you will turn on if you are required to call him "Sir." Some women will not tolerate words like "slut" and "bitch," others can hardly get their juices flowing without hearing some such language. Some gay men thrill to being called "faggots" while others freeze at the sound of the word. It is usually possible to communicate everything about attitude and language by stepping into the role and attitude you like and using the words you prefer. The response from your potential partner will tell you whether you need to be more obvious about this communication. And, if more explicit explanations are needed, either do the explaining, move on to a different partner, or accept the consequences of your silence.

The place of sex in the scene is a big question for some people. If you see a flogging as foreplay and your partner sees sex as something that never takes place in an SM scene context, it is essential that this difference be uncovered up front. If you're being flogged and feeling good about it, then suddenly his fingers are pushing into your cunt, you will be glad (if you are) only because the two of you were clear from the beginning that sex is within the scope of a flogging. Alternatively, you may have agreed – tacitly or explicitly – that sex would be only before, after, not tonight, never, or whatever. Not knowing can be tragic, and this is information which can almost always be communicated understandably without becoming so explicit that you interfere with the spontaneity of the upcoming scene.

Whether the subject is sex or some other factor, attitude is at least as important as the words chosen in maintaining a scene-accommodating atmosphere. If a bottom asks, "Are you going to fuck me when you cut me down?" it can be a shocking scene-ending surprise or totally seductive, depending on timing and tone. Often, though, the difference between successful communication that supports the scene and uncomfortable, even rankling words is attention to the dynamic. "Don't come near me with that damned braided cat-o-nine," will not work as well as, "Sir, nothing would please me more than to be able to take that cat, but I know I'd disappoint you if I tried tonight." In fact, with many Tops, language sprinkled with "Sir" or "Ma'am" just can't go wrong.

Generally speaking, the more private the scene, the more likely that sex or sexual touching is going to be an acceptable. For some reason – or none – a lot of people are able to play and cry and bleed with others watching, but cannot bear to have their breasts or genitals fondled under the same circumstances. It's all purely personal, but the patterns tend to also be common to most members of a given group or circle of players. The "usual" way may be quite local, but being aware of how sexual scenes get in a given setting with a given group can save you a lot of embarrassment or disappointment.

JOB ONE FOR THE TOP

Networking and negotiating are clearly everyone's job, but they are primarily protections for the bottom, and are primarily activities of bottoms. From the perspective of the Top, the main content of the pre-scene activity of networking and negotiating is really the simple process of selecting a partner and seducing that partner's consent. In fact, that seduction of consent is Job One for the Top throughout the interaction, including the actual flogging.

Job One continues as the scene goes on. Once she agrees to do a scene with a particular bottom, the task of the Top is to seduce consent. The first stockpile of consent is usually inspired by mutual attraction. Even if it is expressed in words like, "She could do anything she wants to me," the initial consent is a "limited supply." Consent can be used up. In a good scene, one that pushes the bottom toward the fulfillment of his expectations, the consent is used to nearly nothing any number of times, but new stores of consent are seduced by the Top as the scene progresses.

Various Tops seduce consent in various ways. Being attractive to the potential partner is a beginning. Wearing scene clothing and fetish gear can increase

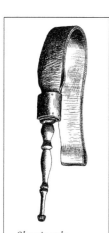

Showing the bottom a particularly tantalizing toy is one way to seduce consent.

the level of consent the scene begins with. Displaying and looking at floggers and whips, talking about them in erotic terms and handling them sensuously can seduce further consent. Then, once the scene is underway, a Top can use whatever she knows about the bottom and his desires to seduce more consent as it is required. Often, the difference between a great scene and one that simply went well is entirely in how closely the action stayed to the brink of expired consent without ever consuming the last un-renewed bit of consent. A scene can also end badly, basically running down rather than playing out, if the consent is consumed so slowly that the bottom is not excited by the interplay of consent and seduction.

To push even a single step beyond the currently existing consent will end the scene or at least end the bottom's enjoyment of the scene. But playing at the edge of consent, at a place where the bottom often enough questions his willingness to go on, keeps a scene very lively and almost insures that it will be a good or even a great experience for both partners.

The skills of the Top are the centerpiece of her seductive abilities. An interesting change of rhythm at just the right moment, a sudden shift from stinging blows to thudding ones, or a change from one instrument to another can all seduce consent from a bottom who may have been getting near the end of his willingness to go on.

Consuming consent only means that the Top is giving the bottom what he has agreed to. Consent is fully consumed if the bottom gets all the stimulation he wants or all that he knows he wants. That's great at the end of a scene. However, by seducing further consent before allowing the scene to collapse for lack of continuing consent, the Top is helping the bottom see his desire for still more stimulation and experience. At the same time, he is promising to provide this newly desired stimulation. It is in this interplay of consuming and seducing consent, giving and monitoring consent that most of what is called the Top-bottom "dynamic" (or even the "power exchange") has its only clear-cut and describable dimensions. While people talk about technical skill more when describing a player, it is the expertise of a Top in Job One that really makes him or her popular and desirable, often even making a far less attractive Top the most desired dominant in a group where other very attractive people get fewer chances to play.

Clothing, Positions and Equipment

A number of questions are brought up and answered as a couple moves into a flogging scene, often without much being noticed. The basic questions have to do with the clothing they will wear or remove, the position in which the body will be maintained during the scene, whether some form of bondage or restraint will be employed, which equipment will be used, whether the bottom will be wear a blindfold, gag or hood, and the body parts likely to be flogged. The answers to these questions are often presumed and accepted without a word being spoken, but they are most successfully "ignored" if both players know what the questions are, at least in general, and what answers are possible. Even a bottom who claims to be prepared for "anything" will have preferences and will consider it "wrong" if the Top's choices vary much from what he would have chosen himself.

Clothing, except for the need to uncover the strike zone, is mostly a question of comfort or erotic charge, but there are other considerations. Certainly, if clothing is needed for warmth, it should be worn, but it would be better to have the SM space warm enough to obviate this concern. And, without a doubt, if certain clothing or gear conveys an erotic charge to either or both people, it should be permitted or encouraged. You do want to think whether the clothing in question might get in the way or create a danger. A corset, for example, may be very sexy, but still be completely inappropriate for either the Top or bottom during a flogging. The constriction of breathing by a corset, for example, could be a significant difficulty for a bottom. Similarly, a corseted Top might find unexpected restrictions on movement that make the shots and movements of the floggers unpredictable.

A special concern for flogging is footgear. The Top may have a lot of latitude in choosing footgear, but very high or very thin heels may be dangerous, if only because they might break. And both the Top and bottom may need support for their ankles – the bottom more than the Top – during a heavy scene. Because joint injuries sometimes take a long time to develop to the point that they actually cause pain, it is not uncommon for someone – especially a bottom – to stress or strain an ankle during a flogging and not recognize a connection between the injury and the scene. In any event, if you know your ankles are weak, you should consider always wearing tightly laced, high-top shoes when being flogged. And, in fact, ankle-supportive footwear is never a mistake.

Clothing can also support or communicate choices that have been made about the place of sex in the scene. Keeping pants or a skirt on, for example, covers the temptation when sexual touching is not intended. Having the ass uncovered for possible flogging can be good, though, even if the scene is meant not to become sexual. The options are all open, and should be seen as choices that are made and in place whether they are discussed or not.

The positioning of the bottom is all too often determined by habit, fantasy, the available spaces or, worst of all, complete ignorance of the fact that position really matters. This is unfortunate. The most commonly used position – the bottom fixed to a Saint Andrew's cross, arms up, legs spread wide – is actually far from optimal for most floggings. Even presuming that the area to be flogged is mainly the upper back, the arms-up position remains, at best, mindless. In consideration of the almost universal use of this posture, it would be wise to understand what is wrong with it, and to consider some alternatives.

Standing, from the floor up then: Spreading the bottom's feet to meet the lower ends of the Saint Andrew's cross is usually wrong because humans are not made of two-by-ten lumber and may tire, strain their groins or just be unnecessarily and unintentionally uncomfortable at that wide a spread. Yes, spreading the feet is a good idea, but the space between the feet should be a balance of comfort and stability, not a measure of the breadth of the cross that happens to be available. On any cross or other equipment, it is possible to set the bottom's feet only as far apart as is right and comfortable. Maybe you will have to ignore or not use built-in restraints, but better that than to have a bottom exhausted and distressed by the posture and not fully "present" for a flogging. For most bottoms, the comfortable, stable and most "invisible" distance for the feet to spread apart is approximately equal to shoulder width. On most equipment and dungeon furniture, this width of the bottom's stance can be accommodated and the

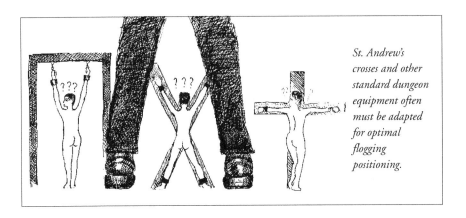

St. Andrew's crosses and other standard dungeon equipment often must be adapted for optimal flogging positioning.

feet can be restrained if necessary, although the restraint will differ with the relative sizes of the bottoms and the equipment.

Of course, the distress of an uncomfortable position maybe a plus for some bottoms. That changes the choices, but it should not be permitted to encourage a position that increases the risk of groin or ankle injury.

Special consideration should be given to the position of the arms of a bottom who is being flogged. To get a full understanding of this question and the best answers to it, have a friend stand in front of you, facing away. For most bodies, especially those with less muscle mass on the back and butt, the shoulder-wide stance of the feet and an arms-down and slightly forward position will give the thickest musculature and the most relaxed muscles on the upper back. If so, these should be considered optimal for the bottom in the scene.

Since striking the body should almost always mean striking muscle (if we mean for the pain to be managed or processed for pleasure's sake), thicker and more relaxed muscles are to be preferred. On the other hand, some bottoms actually are so connected, mentally, to the traditional legs-spread-wide and arms-bound-up posture that the loss of headspace in a more "appropriate" position is "inappropriate." Nonetheless, arms down means more muscle to strike, so it is to be preferred when the scene is going to be longer or more intense than the bottom is accustomed to. In the absence of any compelling reason to bind the arms upward, choose lower bondage points... just in case the scene might last or become intense.

Body angle, meaning how far forward the bottom is leaning, is also often determined by the cross or other equipment in use. Again, there are human factors that are not always adequately considered by the equipment maker or that may be different for the bottom and/or the Top in a given scene. If the bottom has a nice, gripping sole on his boots, maybe the angle is somewhat less important, but if not, he can spend far too much energy and attention just trying not to slide back or strain his ankles. The idea of having the cross there is to support the bottom and have him in place for the Top's attention, but if he's wrestling with the force of gravity trying to slide him back and down, he's not really present for flogging.

Rarely, a cross or other equipment – especially shackles on a wall – will be set up in such a way that there is no room for the bottom to lean forward at all, or no support if he does. This forces too much of the bottom's attention to be spent on the question of hunching forward in some way to "catch" the whip effectively. Given whatever equipment, the angle can be and must be adjusted to give the bottom an easy victory over gravity and to give the Top easy access to the target area. Sometimes, especially with very tall or very short bottoms, you may need to add a box under the feet or to put some kind of padding between the cross and the body parts in contact with it to get an appropriate position.

Equipment varies so much – as do people – that it is impossible to spell out rules. If the subject is considered from both the point of view of the bottom's freedom from concern about holding a position and the Top's clear view and access to the target area, appropriate postures can be achieved in most situations.

Lying down for a flogging has some real advantages. Some Tops have a problem with the concept of the bottom "lying down on the job," and others have a problem managing the angle or posture needed in order to flog a bottom who is lying down. Nonetheless, once the Top's possible objections are answered, this is an option that works extremely well for many bottoms.

All concerns about the angle of the body and the possibility of sliding around or having to fight gravity are completely obviated by having the bottom lie down flat. Bondage becomes both easier and, since the circulation is not being challenged by gravity, less likely to become problematic. The bottom who is lying down can very easily dismiss everything from his or her mind except the incoming sensations.

Of course, lying down does not have to mean lying on the floor, although some Tops prefer to have the bottom on the floor to leave plenty of room for their floggers to move in. Others prefer something in the way of a table (easier bondage) or bed because it requires or encourages less gymnastic positions on the part of the Top. Still others like a bench on which the bottom's back and butt can be presented at bed-height or higher, while the limbs and sometimes even the head are not on the same plane, and are therefore safer from stray strokes.

One advantage of a bottom lying down is that the target areas of the body can be placed and positioned for the Top's convenience, even if there is a significant disparity in the height of the Top and bottom. Another posture that is excellent for flogging and yet seldom used is kneeling. A rug or knee pads may be needed to keep the bottom comfortable enough to bear a flogging while in a kneeling position, but it allows some significant convenience as well. It is obviously one of the postures that can be used to compensate for a height difference between the partners. Kneeling also allows for different bondage options, and easier posture-maintenance for some unrestrained bottoms.

Real pain pigs may prefer arms-up just to get to the hurting more quickly and tough-guy attitudes may cause some bottoms to prefer positions that are more demanding. Other factors of environment or local habit can enter into the calculations as well. And a Top may or may not be comfortable accommodating a bottom's wishes, or in promoting his own at the bottom's "expense." In any case, as always, do it your way, so long as that way is acceptable to the players involved.

Restraints or No Restraints

Most flogging scenes are set up by restraining the bottom to some degree. The Top (and/or the couple) must determine whether to use restraints, how securely to restrain the bottom, what kind of restraints to use, if any.

A flogging with no restraints at all is safe if the bottom is not going to "become involuntary" and risk hurting himself by jumping about out of control. Many bottoms prefer to be unrestrained and many Tops like the sense of the bottom being able to just stay in place and take the beating. However, the risk of the bottom surprising herself and the Top by "running away" from the blows is significant. If the bottom moves, an otherwise safe shot with a whip can become dangerous, especially if the bottom turns around or squats down to any extent while the whip is in the air. A bottom who climbs the equipment can also end up with whip strokes landing on muscles and skin that are not warmed up for action or, worse, landing hard on the kidneys, neck, elbows or other joints. So, there are both "mental-seasoning" and practical reasons for choosing to restrain the bottom. And, alternatively, there are some potentially compelling reasons for not restraining a bottom who wants to prove himself by "taking it like a man," or whatever. The choice should, in any case, a conscious one, the result of consideration, not habit.

Handcuffs are a very poor choice for flogging bondage – their narrowness and harshness increase the chance of damage to the wrists.

Minimal restraint is often all that is needed, and this can be – as with Master Jim and Leila – nothing more than securing the hands. By restraining Leila's hands with her arms, in effect, hugging the St. Andrew's cross, Jim was assured that Leila's range of movement side to side and in turning around was sufficiently limited. This also gave Leila a fairly free range of movement for he feet and legs, meaning she would be able to comfort herself by changing position slightly. What's more, many bottoms use large-muscle movements (often leg movements) to help them process and withstand the stimulation of a flogging, making minimal restraint more effective for them.

Higher degrees of restraint are often desirable if it is known or suspected that the bottom is one who moves around a great deal or jerks from position to position suddenly (as many do), or if the Top is somewhat less experienced. A less experienced Top will be less able to redirect a whip in mid-stroke and, perhaps, less perfect in his or her aim to begin with.

The type of bondage used during flogging will depend on what the bottom is being secured to and other factors, but for purposes of general discussion, a cross will do. Restraining the wrists, whether up or down, whether to the face and edges of the cross or around the cross, is the most basic level. Next, it might be considered useful – for practical or mental reasons – to bind the ankles to the floor-end of the cross. It is advisable to leave some freedom of movement for the feet, but a few inches is enough. And, finally, tying the waist to the middle of the cross is especially useful if the scene is likely to become physically active or the bottom – left unrestrained – is likely to move a great deal. Where possible, it is best to secure the waist by using a broad belt (like a weight lifting belt) with D-rings, tying the rings to the cross. The reason for this is that ropes and narrow belts can become dangerous to the kidneys if the bottom's movement becomes violent. The broad belt can also, incidentally, protect the kidney area from stray whip strokes, of course.

It is usually not a good idea to add other restraints – especially snug rope restraints – to bind the forearms, thighs or calves to the cross. While the binding of the legs probably does not present any special danger, it is not usually needed, and it can limit the bottom's movement to the point of interfering with her ability to manage the stimulation of the flogging. The forearms are another matter altogether. A very wise and experienced bondage Top may choose to tie the arms to the cross. All others are warned against it since the fulcrum-effect of the strong upper arm wrenching the weaker forearm against bindings and the cross can be painfully bruising and may even present the risk of breaking the bones of the forearm or severely straining the wrist joint.

Circulation can also be interfered with when bondage is tight. If blood circulation is not free and pretty much normal, it can lead to lightheadedness or even fainting, but that would be very unusual with the kind of restraint required for flogging. More commonly, a wrist restraint is either installed too snugly or becomes tighter in the course of the scene, resulting in poor circulation in the hand. If the hand is cold or losing color, there is a problem that should be corrected by loosening the restraint. Allowing (ordering?) the bottom to put the cool or colorless hand down for a moment will usually get the blood flowing again. Of course, it would not be out of the way for a Top to take the opportunity to extend her seduction by being extra "helpful" here. Massaging the hand or warming it on her own work-heated body could be a nice touch.

The details of bondage and its possible complications are beyond the scope of this book, but there is a book on the subject: *Jay Wiseman's Erotic Bondage Handbook* (Greenery Press, Emeryville, CA, 2000.)

An alternative to ropes and belts for immobilizing bondage on a cross would be to wrap as much of the bottom's body as possible, enclosing the cross with the body in the bandage, plastic wrap or other bondage material. This makes the bondage an important part of the scene and takes time, which can be either good or bad depending on the situation. But done with care, it gives relatively safe, secure and fully immobilizing bondage that does not interfere with the flogging. This is not usually what is wanted, but it may be "just the thing" sometimes.

Another alternative frequently used would be sets of ready-made restraints. Once you learn rope bondage sufficiently, you will probably prefer the predictability of your own rope restraints over the strap-on leather restraints commonly available and often not in perfect repair in many play spaces.

In the meantime, whatever restraints are used, the same cautions apply and the same vigilance about the restrained body parts is required.

CHOOSING DUNGEON FURNITURE AND EQUIPMENT

Granted, floggers seldom have many choices about the furniture or equipment they will use, even in a large well-equipped dungeon. What's more, with reasonable care and attention, most places with space for the swinging of the whips are acceptable, and just about any equipment can be used.

Experienced players will find it relatively easy to squeeze some kind of flogging scene into just about any available space. With short floggers, sometimes called bedroom whips, it is even possible to do a scene with both players actually on the bed. Generally, however, for a carefree and uncramped flogging, the optimal space would be at least eight feet wide and six feet from the cross or wall where the bottom is to the clear space behind the Top. More space would be luxurious, but is probably not really needed.

This same optimal space for a flogging would also have heat enough to make the bottom comfortable naked and air circulation sufficient to keep the

Top for overheating with the activity. It would also have lighting from overhead near the bottom and from the sides of the space, and would not have any lighting coming from behind the Top. Light that falls on the bottom from behind the Top gives the Top a shadow of each whip to contend with and makes it very difficult to judge exactly when and where the whip will land on the bottom.

No restraints: If the bottom is not being restrained, something to lean on or a chair-back to hold onto might be a good idea, just as an anchor or a point at which to fix attention. In fact, no-restraint bondage is sometimes possible using nothing more than a blank wall. The Top might have the bottom feel around on the wall until her hands come to rest against the wall in places where she says she is comfortable and ready to be flogged. The Top could then draw lines around the "planted" hands – closer to the hands for more sadistic Tops? Then the bottom would be "punished" for the infraction of allowing either hand to leave the outline on the wall. Some bottoms find this a very good method for focusing themselves away from the pain, others find it annoying or even comical. Any of these readings of the circumstances could be desirable or unbearable depending of the people involved and the situation.

Poor choices: When choosing equipment, it is useful to know the reactions of the bottom. A cross that can easily be pushed across the floor may be a poor choice if the bottom likes to thrash around, particularly if he moves his legs much. A piece of equipment that can be tipped over is obviously often a poor choice for flogging. Also, any equipment which can only be used by stretching or straining the bottom's body to meet the needs of the equipment is probably a bad idea. Choose for the bottom's comfort (although it may be un-sexy to say that's what you are doing). This will give the scene the greatest latitude to develop and leave the bottom with the most resources for bearing or processing the pain.

A woman's concern: Some women report that St. Andrew's crosses at specific angles and sizes cause a problem by resulting in the edges of the uprights rubbing their nipples or pressing hard into their breasts. Of course, other women may look forward to this. If it is a problem, it can sometimes be solved by draping towels over the cross beams to provide both padding and a more accommodating surface for sensitive nipples. It is not that unusual to see a leather jacket or vest used in the same way, which may add something to the scene in the way of supporting a bottom's leather fetish.

Whatever equipment you choose for a flogging, be sure the bottom's face, genitals and joints are not going to bang or rub against it unless you are protecting the body adequately or have assessed the possibility of "collateral pain" and found it an acceptable risk.

BLINDFOLDS, GAGS AND HOODS

The use of blindfolds, gags and hoods during flogging is entirely up to the people involved, so long as some clearly understood method of communicating is in place. Safewords are of little use to a bottom who is tightly hooded or has a gag in her mouth.

Some bottoms find that wearing a hood increases their ability to accept a flogging. Others are frightened or overwhelmed by it.

The fetish value or comfort factor for the bottom provided by these items can be very great. It is not at all unusual for a bottom who likes hoods to find his limits much more advanced when he is flogged with a hood on, for example.

Of course, the concerns that would apply to the use of blindfolds, gags and hoods in any circumstances apply when they are part of the preparation for flogging. Most people, for instance, cannot (and should not) wear a snug hood or a blindfold over contact lenses. Many people with dental bridgework or with any kind of removable dental appliances should be wary of gags that actually extend into the mouth. Anyone who has trouble breathing – as with asthma or allergies – will want to be sure their breath is not overly restricted by a hood or gag.

About novices: On the good side of the equation, blindfolds, gags and hoods can be very helpful to bottoms, particularly less experienced flogging bottoms, who are attempting to challenge their own limits by the degree of the flogging. These bottoms often find that they can "go away" from the pain and into the high of the action more easily if they can't see or if they feel free to cry out loudly. Often, this novice-comfort becomes a continuing part of the pleasure of being flogged, too. Other novices may find that being unable to communicate verbally because of a gag or hood is too frightening and interferes with their ability to relax and allow the flogging to take place normally.

PARTS TO FLOG, PARTS TO AVOID HITTING

Which body parts will be flogged is largely a question of preference, but it is also a matter of tremendous importance. Surely, the matter of where not to flog the human body is the most important information about flogging that can be taught.

Jim and Leila chose the most common flogging area, the upper back. The butt and thighs can also be flogged very effectively with the same techniques and tools. A man's chest is a good flogging zone, so long as his face is safe either because it is well protected or because the Top is that accurate. A woman's breasts are not such a good flogging target since repeated bruising of the breast may be implicated in increased cancer risk and other health risks may also be involved. But, some women like to have their breasts flogged, a safety choice that no one can take away from them, so long as they can find partners willing to do the flogging. A history of cystic breasts represents a relatively immediate danger, and most assuredly should mean not permitting breast flogging. Breast implants are another issue. For most women with most breast implants, flogging of the breasts should simply not take place. If you have implants and can discuss flogging with your doctor, you may discover that you are one of the rare women who has less than usual reason to be concerned. If you are unsure, don't do it!

Even the genitals, male and female, can be flogged with the right whips, a reasonable concern for safety and the right circumstances. Genital flogging, of course, is far more risky than the whipping of the upper back or ass, but it is not as dangerous as it sounds… for careful people!

There are actually two areas of concern when it comes to the question of which body parts are not to be flogged.

Question #1: The first question is often seen as mere preference – which it often is – but it can be very important. It is the psychological response of the bottom (and perhaps the Top) when a particular area of the body is beaten. A person with personal fears or traumatic memories of non-erotic punishment, for example, may have trouble withstanding a scene that resembles the feared or remembered punishment. This sometimes makes the butt off-limits since spanking, switching, caning and beating of the ass are more or less usual ways that parents/adults punish (or abuse) children. There can be other reasons for fearing or having emotionally charged reactions to the beating of certain body parts, some of them purely irrational, but none of them cured or abolished by being ignored. These seldom have to be explained. A bottom can just say, "It won't work for me if you..." and this is usually sufficient.

Question #2: The second area of concern about where not to flog is actual physical safety. It is generally unsafe to flog where there is no muscle to absorb the blow. That simple statement covers most of the body parts that are best left either off-limits or flogged only by an expert who knows exactly what he or she is doing and why. More specifically, hands and feet, elbows and knees, the neck and head, the belly and, very especially, the lower back over the kidneys are usually inappropriate areas for flogging. Blows to the lower back can also be dangerous and painful in an entirely wrong way – besides the danger of kidney damage – because the spine is relatively unprotected there. It is commonly said that the spine should not be flogged, but this is a relatively meaningless statement on its face. Of course, the spine is included in the prime area of the upper back, but it is protected by being in a channel between the muscles of the right and left sides of the back. Direct blows with a heavy whip that fall entirely between the muscle mounds of the back may in fact present some slight danger but, if so, injuries of this kind are inexplicably unreported.

The spine in the lower back does not have the protection of being in a channel of muscles. So, if there is reason to be concerned that blows may fall in this area, a weight-lifting belt or other protection would be a good idea.

The good news, in a sense, is that flogging the heavier muscles is both easier for the Top and more pleasurable for the bottom than flogging any of the areas that are dangerous or inadvisable. The upper back naturally catches whip strokes and deflects them away from the lower back of most people in most postures. The thighs are more readily reached than the ankles. The ass stands out – some might say "just begging to be hit" – from the body in such a way as to be easily targeted.

With soft enough strokes of light enough whips, of course, the risk of injury to even such areas as the elbows and backs of the knees is reduced to nearly nothing. On the other hand, it is hard to imagine how these strokes to areas without the pad of muscle to warm to the pain can be erotic for anyone. Perhaps in a genuine torture scene or an heavy interrogation scene, blows to these muscle-free, injury-prone areas would make some sense, but great care would have to be taken not to actually damage the bones, joints or tendons.

Similarly, as mentioned above, appropriately careful whip strokes at a reasonable level of intensity can be used on the genitals. In fact, some bottoms develop a capacity to bear and enjoy the sharp bite of a single-tail whip or the crushing blows of very heavy floggers on their genitals. Such bottoms are relatively few, however, and it can never be assumed that a bottom, just because he does other heavy scenes, is ready for such activity. Nor should a Top without experience in genital flogging assume that it is safe just because he has seen the bottom he is now playing with bear such attention from another Top at another time.

When flogger tails trail onto the neck, it is seldom a great concern beyond the fact that the skin there is not warmed up and the sting of the blow will not be easily processed by the bottom. A direct blow to the neck, on the other hand, may be very dangerous and must be avoided. If there is a place where the spine itself is in danger of injury from blows of a whip or flogger, it is in the area of the neck. Again, it is easy to provide protection if you are concerned. Draping a towel or article of clothing around the neck, for example, can be worked into the preparation for the scene without reducing the erotic charge.

In the same way, while there is little reason for concern about actual injury, flogger tails trailing onto the ribs, wrapping out of the warmed-up area, will sometimes give a shocking (rather than pleasurable) pain. Similar unwanted effects will be caused if the flogger crosses off the back onto the arms or armpits or if it lands in any unexpected area. Areas that have not been warmed up will often swell or blister from the single blow they do receive. This is particularly true when the wrapping or stray stroke involves a single flogger tail snapping into the area. In the discussion about "leathering up" of flogged skin later in this book the explanation will become clear.

Every bottom is different. People are remarkably individual and even stunningly unique with regard to the reception they will give to surprising wraps and unexpected shots of the flogger tails. Some bottoms actually look forward to the "wake-up" effects of "wrapping" and even direct blows to unprepared areas. Some couples also distinguish flogging for erotic purposes from what they consider flogging for "punishment." The latter purpose might be better served, for some people, by blows to less muscled or unprepared areas, but this can not be advised for most flogging scenes.

STING AND THUD: WHAT A WHIP FEELS LIKE

Even on the most appropriate body areas, where the muscle is thick enough to absorb a whip stroke and the stimulation can be welcomed by most bottoms, there is a question to be considered. It is usually framed as the preference for "sting" or "thud."

Sting is pretty easily understood. A whip stroke stings if the stimulation it delivers remains largely on the skin. A superficial pain that bites or tingles is called sting, and is generally harder for most bottoms to process into the desired pleasure than the more penetrating or thudding blows of denser whips. In general, stingy strokes tend to make a sharp, red mark if they are landed heavily enough, while heavy thudding strokes leave an area reddened but not striped.

While some floggers and whips would be rated as all-sting or as all-thud by all bottoms, many are described – especially when used with a lighter touch – differently by different bottoms. And, when used lightly, it is true that some floggers spread to the point that the blow is actually landed as many separate contact points, each providing a sting, while the tails of the same flogger moving fast enough will gather together and land a single thudding blow.

Most bottoms agree that long sessions of sting can eventually lead to a kind of pain that they are able to process and welcome, but many bottoms are, to put it mildly, not that patient. However, thud is another matter. For many bottoms, thud is not pain at all, but something in the massage-like range of stimulation. For some thud becomes "painful" only much later, when the muscle is bruising, after the bottom's hormones have kicked in to the point that they handle it very easily anyway.

To describe what is usually or always sting or thud in any real detail is complex and so rife with differences of opinion in all directions that it is probably also pointless. However, a few statements can be made that are likely to be generally (if not universally) accepted: Denser materials tend to thud while less dense materials tend to sting. Blows to smaller areas of skin are more likely to sting than blows that fall over a broader area. Harder instrument surfaces are more likely to land with a sting and less hard or less smooth surfaces will sting less.

Also, of course, any given whip or flogger can be used in ways that create sting, as when a very rapid pass, even with a light "thuddy" flogger, snaps just its tips into the skin. But many instruments are completely incapable of producing a thudding blow.

Gauging the sting-thud quotient: Density in flogger materials may be hard to judge, but it can be assessed roughly by lifting the tails of the flogger on the fingers and giving them a squeeze. Denser materials are heavier for their size/volume and they "give" less when squeezed. Taking this physical assessment into consideration, add in the size of the pattern of the landed tails (tighter or smaller area equaling more sting). Then include the nature of the surface of the tails as the least important sting-thud qualifier. You get some idea of what to expect this way, but the real test of any instrument is easy. Hit yourself with it and you will know how it feels. Guessing or deducing sting-thud is always a choice among unconfirmed assumptions and can be completely wrong, particularly with some of the non-leather and even space program spin-off materials from which floggers are being made. Some forms of Neoprene and Teflon and the new, high-density plastics can be especially surprising.

THE ELEMENTS OF FLOGGING

Networking to find a partner, negotiating to arrange a mutually desirable scene, monitoring the progress of the action by being aware of the feedback loops between the partners, selecting appropriate instruments at the right times to produce the desired effects and seeing that the scene comes to a safe and satisfying end... these are the elements of a flogging. Most of these elements have been observed in the interaction between Leila and Master Jim. Others will be seen more completely in other scenes described in later chapters.

SCENE TWO

DENNIS AND MARK AT HOME

DENNIS AND MARK HAVE WHAT THEY BOTH believe will be a long-term relationship, although they have been together as Master and slave for only a year so far. In the beginning of their relationship, mark was less experienced in SM overall, but Dennis was less experienced with floggers. For Dennis, mark learned to bottom in long-term bondage scenes. For mark, Dennis has put in hours whacking pillows and drawing boot-polish stripes on the walls with floggers and other whips. Dennis has also taken a couple of classes about flogging at a local club and allowed an experienced flogging Top to critique his style. He has even bottomed to a very good Top to get a clear idea of what a flogging "is." All along, the men have practiced together (and with others) the favorite scenes each of them brought to the relationship. Tonight, Dennis will flog mark with no bondage. The scene is a special one since Dennis usually demands bondage since that's what turns him on, or "traditionally" has been.

So, this is a kind of graduation for Dennis and a treat for mark.

SM headspace is important to both men, and they've discovered that they are each able to get into the right space easiest by way of a little ritual they developed soon after they got together. It was no one's plan, but it works. When they feel the time to go into the dungeon is near, they become quiet and separate for at least a few minutes. When he is ready, Dennis goes to his favorite chair, a huge over-stuffed easy chair that mark gave him. He stretches out, his feet extended on the rug in front of the chair, his head dropped back almost as if he is sleeping. When mark is ready and finds his Master in this pose, it is irresistible for him to service the man's boots, kissing and licking them as both a sign of his submission and an exercise of a mutually enjoyed fetishistic pleasure. He works on the boots for several minutes before licking his way up denim or leather or whatever to bring his head to rest in his Master's crotch. After a few silent minutes, one or the other will move or make a sound. If the other is also ready to go, they rise – without further communication – and mark crawls to the dungeon, closely following Dennis's boots.

Tonight they are so in tune with one another that neither knows who moved first.

In the dungeon, mark stands at the end of the room, holding on to the multipurpose, floor-to-ceiling chains stretched 15 to 20 inches from the wall. Tonight's flogging will be less affectionate, or less obviously affectionate, than most of their scenes. They've discussed it and determined that Dennis will be best able to approach and possibly even challenge mark's pain-tolerance limits – something both men hope for – by remaining a little more than usually "tough" and stereotypically "Toppish." (They know for sure that indulging their natural inclination to become physically affectionate leads them to behave more gently with each other.)

Both men are clear about the many intentions of the scene they are undertaking, including the fact that it will be an exchange of the kind they call making love, however violent it may appear.

Dennis has his floggers arranged on hooks on the wall beside himself. He takes a moment to choose a flogger that is very weighty for him but not terribly heavy as a pain-giver. It is a 72-tail, garment leather flogger with a thick, lead-wrapped handle. It is not the softest or lightest whip in the growing collection, but it can be gentle enough to do warm-up. He starts the flogging with a few very light strokes that really amount to nothing more than swinging the tails of the flogger into the air and letting them drop, brushing mark's skin in their free-fall. This does little more than inform mark which whip they have begun with and give Dennis a chance to ease into the Top headspace by drinking in the scene: boy, whip, dungeon... all of it.

Soon, Dennis speeds up the movement of the flogger enough to be able to control it in a series of figure-eight and vertical-plane strokes which actually begin the flogging in earnest. He sees the pink whip marks raised on the boy's skin and sees them, at first, fade very quickly. After a few minutes, they don't fade so quickly and, a few minutes further along, they stop appearing as separate marks. The skin of mark's back is becoming pink or red all over, puffing up very slightly as the physical reaction to the "trauma" of the flogging generalizes in the area. This is the purpose of the warm-up, and it is working perfectly. The boy's back is "leathering up," signaling that his body is reacting completely normally to the flogging.

Still, the warm-up strokes don't last very long, ten or fifteen minutes at most. Then Dennis picks up a second flogger. This one has fewer tails, but they are made of a thicker leather. At first, Dennis grips both floggers in the same hand, swinging and landing them together. He knows that mark is unable to identify the mixed tails as any one instrument in their dungeon. To a certain extent, his very purpose at the moment is to free mark of his habit of identifying and internally commenting on the whips – to allow him to let go more than he usually does.

After a minute or less of various strokes with the two floggers together, Dennis switches to circular, overhead strokes, his forearm passing over his own head, swinging around to brush the flogger heavily across mark's back as it rushes into another helicopter-blade circle. With the earlier strokes, he landed only two or three of each five strokes, allowing the whip to just "kiss" mark's back or to pass without touching on the other strokes. With the overhead stroke, he lands every pass, each shot a little heavier than the one before. Then, at an angle and in a fashion he has actually practiced and planned very carefully, Dennis lets go of the garment-leather flogger and continues to work with only the heavier one.

Dennis barely notices his success at flinging the lighter flogger through the open double-wide doorway and onto the sofa. He continues flogging mark with overhead strokes, tipping the plane of the stroke one way and then the other, higher on the right, then on the left. Soon, putting the power of both arms into the flogger, he is beating mark's back with level strokes, baseball-bat style. These controlled, level blows start with the flogger tails flung back, then they move in a semicircle forward, stopping just after the point of contact. No energy is wasted completing a circle before the flogger is drawn back for another stroke. The follow-through of this stroke frequently involves the tails landing painlessly on Dennis's upper arm, the one he has turned toward mark. He doesn't mind. Drawing the flogger into position for each stroke is very much like a baseball player swinging his bat into place: down across the "home plate" the tails swing, then up with increasing force until they "pull up" straight in the air. At that point, the blow must begin immediately before the tails slow down enough to respond to gravity – crumpling into each other and hanging down limp.

Every shot is jolting mark, and every contact is met with a rattling of his support chains and a bestial grunt. It takes Dennis a moment to notice that *he*, not mark, is making the unanswered animal noises. Somehow, his awareness that mark is still silent spurs him to deliver still harder, sharper blows which he is able to do by moving back only slightly, to land a smaller section of the flogger tails on mark's back, but with increasing force. As the amount of energy he puts into the whip is increased, the flogger tails snap slightly as they unfurl against mark's back. This snap – not unlike the cracking of a single-tail whip – increases the sensation level delivered far beyond the increase in Dennis's physical effort.

After a few minutes of jarring blows, Dennis is moved to try getting mark's vocal motor running by using the broadest-landing strokes he knows how to make. He kneels behind the boy and, without missing a rhythmic hit, switches to strokes that he throws up on one side of the back or the other, clapping the widely spread, slow-moving tails almost soundlessly against the near-shoulder mound of muscle with a last-minute tug that puts the energy into the movement without giving the tails time to gather tightly before hitting. At the very moment of contact, he stops moving the flogger handle at all and just allows the tails to trickle down the back, fully splayed and alternately sticking or sliding on the well-worked skin. By the fifth or sixth such stroke, Dennis hears a low humming noise that follows the rippling flogger tails across the red flesh. After several more shots from his kneeling position, every one of them met by a sustained, pleasured purr, Dennis stands and returns to a simple figure-eight stroke, not much more forcefully landed than they were at the very beginning of the scene. Without changing his stroke, he changes whips so deftly mark doesn't notice the little gap in the rhythm of the action. Now, with the same force and energy, with the same motion, Dennis is delivering a much more biting sensation because the tails of the new whip are made of dense, hard, "vinyl-like" rubber. The tails would sting horribly even for mark, but their cutting edges and hard, smooth surface are just what is called for on his hot, leathered-up back.

At first, the figure-eight brushes lightly on the right, the left, the right of mark's back, then it crashes into the left side. This pattern is repeated several times before it shifts. After a heavy blow on the left side of mark's back, Dennis lets the hard rubber flogger brush down the right, left, right, left, then land with a snapping force on the right side of mark's back.

As the speed and force of the whip action increase, Dennis sometimes spaces the heaviest blows further apart with more of the lighter ones, but overall, the action is getting heavier despite the modulation of softer and harder strokes. As the strength he is putting into the heaviest strokes begins to reach the maximum effort he is able to put into the whip's flight, Dennis plays more and more freely with the rhythms and contours of the strokes. For several strokes at a time, he pulls back so that the whip doesn't touch mark at all. Instead, it breezes by, pushing only air against the hot, sensitive skin. These air-strokes eventually take over the scene, faster and harder strokes, none of them landing, are filling the room with the sound of whirring flogger tails and allowing both men to hear their own heavy breathing. Dennis steps in very slightly again, and the strokes connect, every one of them. Each stroke is a body-blow, the heaviest ones hard enough to slam mark into the wall, but he holds tight to the chains and stands his ground.

Sweating and growling, Dennis drops the rubber flogger on the floor and falls on mark like a lion going in for the kill. His short nails and light slaps would hardly have been felt on mark's skin before the flogging, but now the slaps cause mark to jump and the nails leave thin, quickly-disappearing, white lines in the angry flesh and send chills coursing through the boy's body. Each searing white stripe lasts only a second, but it is long enough for Dennis to lunge at it, biting the toughened skin with a wide-open mouth. He is thrilled to hear sharp cries of pained pleasure from mark at every scratch-and-bite combination.

After a dozen or more encounters with his Master's teeth and nails, mark is gasping and verbalizing loudly, but he is not really speaking. He is trembling, his thighs are shuddering, but he holds the chains, pulling at them as if to bring them together in front of himself. The movement and tension in mark's arms stretch his back "open," a very positive signal that is not lost on Dennis.

Slowly, allowing all his nails and his teeth to drag across his lover's skin, Dennis raises himself off the back. As he lifts away, he notices the clear fluid "weeping" through the skin and catching the light here and there all over mark's back. He can't resist the urge to run his hands over the hard planes of the tortured muscles. As he strokes the hot flesh with one hand, he reaches with the other for a narrow, hardwood paddle.

The first paddle strokes are cold imitations of the light slaps and slow rubbing Dennis had been doing with his hand. Then the paddle seems to come to life. Suddenly, Dennis is tapping wildly at mark's back in bursts of 15 to 20 rapid-fire strokes, each outburst separated from the next by a few inches of hard, orange-peel-looking skin and maybe one full second. Before long, he is switching between bursts of paddle strokes and blows with the side of his fist, sometimes throwing in a heavy slam with his entire forearm. Harder and harder, fist and paddle, the blows are eventually being answered by deep, guttural groans. And, as each groan trails off, mark stamps one booted foot in a hesitant but insistent way.

Dennis stops and steps back. He drops the paddle and gives himself a recovery moment. Meantime, mark is recovering too. He stomps quietly, more concerned to move his leg and foot for reasons he doesn't even try to understand than to make a sound putting the foot down. Then Dennis takes a braided cat-o-nine tails from the wall.

The cat bites hard into the richly reddened skin every time it is thrown hard enough to gather its knotted tails together. Even these biting strokes are no challenge to mark at this point. His nearly overheated body welcomes the attention, devours it, sends the sensations racing around from muscle to muscle, and they set off blinding sparks in his mind. It's all welcome. It's what he wants more than anything by now.

Droplets of fluid are weeping through the skin of mark's back after each stroke. Right, left, in a tight, fast figure-eight, the cat sails through its course, drawing the clear but darkening fluid out of the skin. Some of the weeping is translucent pink now, some is darker, some droplets are actually blood, building up and beginning to run down mark's back. Areas are changing colors, too, as bruises form at the sites of the heaviest strokes. And every bruise is sure to have a few drops of blood forming at its edges.

Dennis accelerates his pace and puts more energy into throwing the cat. He also becomes acutely aware of his aim, carefully targeting with each blow an area of his boy's back that is fully "leathered up," but not yet bruised or bleeding. He switches to a hard, snapping throw from overhead and increases the force again. Then, feeling himself, in some emotional way, almost lift off like a helicopter, Dennis stops completely.

The scene is not over. Dennis watches mark's body shudder and tremble for a moment. He can tell from the shivering shoulders that mark is sobbing, but he hears nothing more than a wet in-breath from time to time. As his head clears, Dennis looks over the canes and sjamboks in an umbrella stand near his feet. He chooses a heavy rattan cane, never previously used, and slices through the air with it. If mark is still able to hear and care about such things – which is doubtful – he will know what is coming. In fact, in some vague but important way, even now, he *will* know.

Dennis moves up very close behind his lover, close enough to extend a hand and actually feel the heat radiating from the boy's body. Then closer still, until that heat can be registered on the hot, sweaty skin of his chest. He draws a line or two on mark's back with the cane, pressing its length into the flogged and swollen flesh and drawing it away until its tip draws a wet, white track in the back. The pink-white lines disappear quickly in the canvas of bruises and redness. Then, letting his fingertips just touch mark's waist, Dennis raises the cane over his head and slashes into the waiting back.

The blow collapses mark's body, making him look like a balloon suddenly deflating, although it feels to the boy as though it has pushed him over a cliff into thin air. He doesn't cry out at all. Instead, he breaths in loudly, stuttering the breath deep into his lungs, inflating his body again, sliding his hands up the chains till he is standing full-height again. As he rises, his shoulders push back, creasing and folding his back along the line of his spine.

Dennis waits for at least 15 or 20 seconds as mark drifts in a sea of contradictory emotions – anger, desire, hurt and power are struggling with gratitude, peace, joy and vulnerability – until he is finally able to relax his shoulders and spread his back "open" to his Master completely. Without words, he has prompted Dennis to strike again. He shifts his feet for stability as Dennis raises the cane.

There are just five slashing strokes of the cane before mark lets himself crumble to the floor, turning as he sinks and letting go of the chains. He ends up spread on the floor, belly down, his face buried against his Master's boots, his arms stretched out to painfully and tightly embrace them.

Now mark is crying with a gentleness that surprises Dennis. In little breaks from the grieved tears, mark breathes in deeply and slowly, stretching his whole torso to enclose as much air as he can.

For several minutes, Dennis stands there swaying, his eyes closed, his mind blank, his heart overflowing, as mark continues to wrap himself more and more tightly around the boots. Dennis feels that he is being held up; mark feels that he is being kept from drifting away altogether. As mark's meditative breathing slowly returns to normal, he lets go of the boots and fumbles his hands up Dennis's legs, pulling himself to a kneeling position. "Thank you, Sir," he whispers, drawing Dennis's fingers to his mouth and kissing them.

"Thank you, boy," Dennis whispers, probably far too faintly to be heard, but mark hears it anyway.

SCENE TWO EXAMINED

INNER AND OUTER TECHNIQUES

IN THIS SCENE, THE TOP AND BOTTOM used a familiar, even formal, method to achieve the desired headspace, then used a variety of instruments in several different ways. The informative "feedback loop" between the partners was established, a reminder that, after networking and negotiating, the third communication necessity for flogging (or any pain scene) is feedback.

THE HEAD-SPACE QUESTION

Different people have very different ideas about mental preparation. Leila and Jim in an earlier chapter achieved the adjustment they wanted in a completely free-form, do-it-your-way style. And Leila's primary concern was to feel herself "up to" Jim's attention. Dennis and his boy mark have a different approach. They know each other, and they are playing at home, so they don't have the head-space support that comes from being in a place dedicated to SM scenes at a time when everyone is expected to take advantage of that dedication. In both cases, however, a shift of gears took place before the first blow. If it does not, a flogging can take a long time to get started, and the action required puts a great deal of pressure on both parties to communicate clearly the moment when the "real" action has begun or can begin.

What headspace is and how it is achieved is an extremely individual matter. Many SM players disregard the entire question and suffer no noticeable loss for their choice. Maybe this is sometimes possible because these people "get there" so easily they don't even notice. Others, probably most people, notice the process, but don't have to do anything special to bring it about. They turn on sexually, and they're ready to go. But some people have to think about getting into the right headspace. For them, it is essential to first know what the right headspace is.

It may be best or at least easiest, however, to think what the right SM headspace is not. It is not just wondering if you can bear the upcoming pain. That attitude of testing oneself is unfair to the Top. The equivalent attitude in a Top, of course, is for him or her to start the scene wondering if he or she has the necessary skill or stamina. Again, this is not fair… unless it is clearly communicated in advance, and the bottom finds it an acceptable basis for the scene. Similarly, it is seldom enough to just turn that dial a notch to knowing that you can bear it and stand by waiting for the pain to come, take its toll, and be over with. While "taking it like a man" or "taking what's coming to you" may be a thought pattern that leads some people into the right headspace, it is not a realistically useful headspace in and of itself.

The essential thing about the right headspace – the attitude that opens all options to the max in SM – is a readiness to let go enough to have the scene unfold as it will and to ride, rather than drive, the energy wave. Yes, many people will argue with this and have very different opinions, and it is no one's place to demand any specific mental state of anyone else (except one's own partner of the moment). Nonetheless, it is the experience of many SM players that letting go is *the* important factor. This is not a matter of the bottom instantly resigning responsibility nor of the Top failing to accept responsibility. It is a matter of both partners maintaining their respective degrees and areas of responsibility for themselves and for each other's pleasure, while also being willing to let the *scene* have a life of its own.

No number of words is going to make that clear, but your experience will bear it out quickly.

Fantasy scenes and role-playing games are specific kinds of headspace. Fantasy and role-game scenes could be anything: the Headmaster and the naughty schoolgirl, the Great White Hunter and Tarzan, the Boss Lady and the nervous middle-manager, or what you will. Any such definition of the places of the players in relation to one another can supply ample material for the people involved to develop functional attitudes quickly. This works, of course, to the extent that they are able to let go of their usual roles and attitudes for the sake of the scene. The concept of fantasy scenes seems to be something that is either attractive to a person or not, and very few people can *learn* to enjoy them if the pleasure isn't already there in anticipatory fantasy.

Relationships, whether casual or intimate, can either help or hinder the achievement of the right headspace for a flogging. Lovers, for instance, may know each other so well that they have trouble either entering a fantasy role or even slipping into appropriate degrees of dominance or submission. They can also carry the details of their lives into the scene ("You served my coffee cold" or "You forgot our anniversary"), which is another area where letting go works and not letting go definitely gets in the way. People who are familiar with each other in another context – shoe salesman and customer in real life, for example – may find that starting from their real-life relationship works for (Is the shoe salesman the bottom?) or against (Oh, he's the Top!) the right head space. So, either letting go or embracing and twisting the existing relationship may be appropriate.

Whatever else is true about headspace, the main truth is that it is seldom appropriate to ignore it, and never damaging to consider it. And still, each player has to find his or her own way to get ready for SM ecstasy.

TOYS, TOOLS, INSTRUMENTS FOR FLOGGING

The language with which leatherfolk describe the devices they use in scenes can be very confusing. Some refer to all their SM gear as toys. Others are uncomfortable with that word – and sometimes with calling SM "play," as well – so they choose to say tools or instruments. The arguments can be very persuasive on all sides, and they do matter, but only in the sense that everyone gets to be right… for himself. That is, each SM participant needs to express her or his own attitude in whatever way and in whatever words will work. As the least charged and most neutral term, "instruments" will be used as the generic term here.

The same proliferation of various words for the same thing is expressed when specific instruments are spoken of. A single given instrument may be called a cat, cat-o-nine, cat-o-nine tails, flogger, braided flogger, knotted whip, punishment flogger, and so on. To accommodate these variations, no detailed definitions are given here, nor are any words used as the names or descriptors of flogging instruments here meant to be exclusive. The idea here is to describe processes, instruments and possibilities without entering into arguments about words. A vain attempt in a book, perhaps, but it will work if the reader joins in the charade and accepts that the words used are conveniences.

The common instruments used for flogging are floggers and cats of various descriptions, with a few quirts and novelty whips thrown in to personalize the scenes.

- *Floggers*, here, are generally understood to be instruments (whips) that have a handle and multiple tails, usually flat, braided or not. The horsehair whip may sometimes be called a flogger as well, although in most scenes it is referred to separately as a "horsehair whip"

The instrument on the left is a flat-tailed flogger of very soft leather, such as doeskin or kidskin. The center one is a flat-braided flogger, and the one on the right is a round braided cat. Their sensations are completely different, yet each might play an important part in a good flogging scene.

for clarity. The special quality of floggers is the extremely wide range of possible configurations, materials, etc. in which they can be produced.

- *Cats* are commonly understood to be instruments with braided, compressed or otherwise more dense tails than the simple flogger. The fact that they will have fewer tails is a matter of necessity. The surfaces of rough or braided tails, such as we usually have on a cat, do not glide as smoothly over one another as do tails cut from a single piece of leather. So, if there are too many of them or they are too closely gathered together, they will tangle and be unmanageable. The fact that the usual number of tails is nine, resulting in the cat-o-nine tails, would seem to be an accident of the history of rope making. The most common lay (twisting of the elements) of ropes involves three major bundles of three component bundles each, with these being made up of three worsted cords each. Thus, when the rope is "unlaid" completely, it has 27 strands. When the strands are braided back together to create a cat, the result is nine tails. Apart from the historical and fantastical appeal of cats, they are usually what players "step up to" from simple floggers.

- *Quirts* are the most common "other" instruments (that are still whips of a sort) used in flogging. The name quirt (from Spanish *corto*, short, as in short whip) evolved in the Western U. S. where the Spanish-style whip was used more than the English riding crop by horsemen.

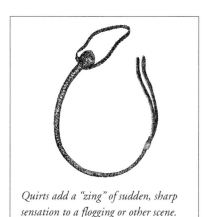

Quirts add a "zing" of sudden, sharp sensation to a flogging or other scene.

A quirt commonly has a rigid or near-rigid handle of at least one foot and a lash of up to two feet. The lash is most usually split down the middle, resulting in two tails. The most treasured quality of the quirt, outside its horse-control history, is the extreme accuracy of targeting that is possible with it, allowing a Top to pinpoint a spot to strike (or avoid). This tightly focused strike zone also means that the quirt is a good instrument for introducing a pain-element into non-flogging scenes.

- *Novelty whips and other instruments* in the whip category are everywhere, and the creativity of contemporary whip makers is coming up with new variations every day. Some of the other instruments used in flogging are the *stock whip*, a longish handle with an elbow before the lash which may be single, split or multiple tails; the *riding crop*, a longish handle with a tag, tab or very short lash at the action end; and a wide range of recent inventions and historic replicas in other configurations. (Note: Single-tailed whips, not properly the domain of this book, are covered to some extent separately at the end of this chapter.)

Horsehair makes a "special effects" flogger that has pride of place in many tops' toybags.

- *Very personal additions to the flogging arsenal* are almost universal. That is, most flogging Tops make use of their hands, fists, forearms, teeth, nails, fingers (as in pinching), whiskers or stubble, tongue (as in licking) and even their chests (as in slamming into the bottom's whole back at once) to extend the range of sensations they can produce. This personal touch

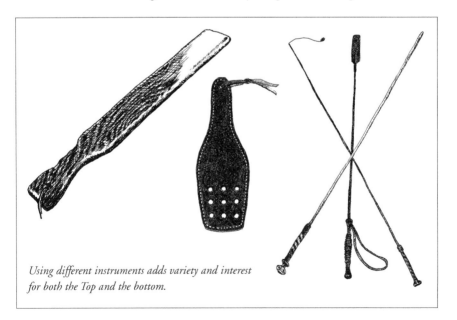

Using different instruments adds variety and interest for both the Top and the bottom.

is often also helpful in Job One, seducing consent, by reestablishing a direct contact between the Top and the bottom. And, as a matter of fact, it can also serve as a sometimes essential reminder to the Top that the bottom is a human being, not a senseless pillow or pillar.

- *Pervertibles* – a name apparently coined by david stein – are very useful. Pervertibles are objects clearly intended for another, usually non-kinky purpose, which can be pressed into service for an SM scene. Among the most clearly flogging-friendly pervertible items are the belt, leather vest, leather pants or shirt. Although no instruction is likely to be needed in converting (or perverting) these items, a little careful experimentation might be in order. Another fun addition to a flogging scene is a towel, usually wet, but possibly interesting dry if it is heavy enough. Certainly most boys get plenty of training and practice in the stinging swat of a wet towel, from both ends of the towel, in the high school locker room. Girls apparently get the same experience in the kitchen at home or school. Gender roles changing as they are in our times, maybe these venues have reversed or become mixed, or (horrors) perhaps schools have outlawed the wet towel fight.

With care, all kinds of items found in the home, hotel room, park or other improvised dungeon can become flogging pervertibles. The care required is a simple matter of being sure that the item works safely and has no unintended effect. Long branches of nettles, for example, can be great fun, but the side-effects can be shocking: blisters, even on the Top's forearms and hands (use gloves and caution); long-lasting itching from the embedding of the stinging fibers in the bottom's skin (unavoidable if they are much used); oily or damp spots around the room which can cause reactions days or weeks later (clean-up is everything). So, like many pervertibles, using nettles requires a good deal of special training, which is a reminder that *most* common items are not as easily bent to perverted use as they may appear to be. Other surprising pervertibles might include adjusting rods from venetian blinds. They invite you by their shape and size to use them to strike a bottom's butt or back, but they can break very easily. Far worse, they sometimes shatter and send sharp splinters of plastic across the room. Some modern plastic hairbrushes can cling or even grab the skin by suction and become extremely painful.

Great care and experimentation is advised with the perverting of any item not intend for SM, but you should also *allow* yourself to experiment and be creative.

- *Belts:* they are used pretty widely in all kinds of SM scenes, usually doubled in half and used in the fashion of a club, but with their own distinctive range of sensations. When doubling a belt, except in very special cases or when your instincts lead you to disregard popular wisdom, turn the studs (if any) to the inside of the fold and keep the buckle-end in your hand. In the long-forgotten days of the 1960s, leathermen often wore studded belts, just as they do today, but no one ever *said* "studded belt." Instead, the men (maybe women, too, even then) said their belts were either plain (no studs) or loaded. The studding was not meant to be decorative. Calling it a "load" was and honest statement: the metal was meant to make the belt heavier and add a good deal of "authority" to the range of sensations it could be used to produce. History aside, the fact is that a belt should almost never be turned so that the studs actually strike the bottom. The rare pain-pig will, nonetheless, demand this special attention, but it is still a relatively dangerous activity.

  Belts can also be used in flogging without doubling them up. With a little practice, a figure-eight stroke (discussed later) can be done with a belt in such a way that the tip, or the last few inches of the belt, land with tremendous accuracy and "authority."

Unwanted pains: In most cases, with most bottoms, it is not useful to supply another type of pain while doing a flogging. Tit clamps pinching at the nipples and ball weights hanging from a guy's testicles tend to be more distracting than enhancing. Of course, a Top of a certain stripe may prefer the distraction which will make the bottom work all the harder to achieve any pleasure from the scene. And, obviously, bottoms of a certain stripe will also want to maximize the painful stimulation, and will be perfectly happy to have multiple flavors of pain to cope with.

End-game instruments for floggings can go two distinct directions. On the one hand, it is possible to compose a flogging such that the last instrument is one step or several steps down from the peak of the scene. This gives a kind of cool-down effect, tucking the end of the flogging back into the "real world" in which the scene began. More often, the end-game instrument is the most intense pain-provider in the scene, pushing the scene to a finale that is a full-scale crescendo, as was the case with Dennis and mark.

In the latter case, there are still two possible processes in effect.

The heavy instrument at the end can be a kind of punctuation. "Here, possibly at your limits, bottom, we are stopping!" is the message in one case. The Top is fully commanding the end of the scene in this situation, and is pushing to consume the current stock of consent on the way out. It works.

In the other use of a heavy instrument, the Top is playing and reading the responses of the bottom, possibly still seducing consent, definitely consuming all allowed consent about as fast as it is given. When a Top, for example, has a bottom count – as Master Jim had Leila count – or gives the bottom a full measure of recovery time between strokes at the end – as Dennis did with mark – the effect is that the end of the scene is about finishing the bottom's "trip."

Counting is the more obvious choice if the Top is intending to give the bottom the freedom to end the scene in the best possible state by her own choice, particularly with a phrase like "only count the good ones." If the bottom is beyond the level of mental control at which counting is possible or reasonable, the Top just has to watch closely, and read the bottom (discussed below) to know which stroke is the last "good one."

The instruments used for this end-game can include canes, heavy cats, sjamboks, narrow paddles and just about anything that is highly controllable. Often, the Top will choose to use an instrument that would have been too intense or too stingy for the bottom earlier.

THE ATTRIBUTES OF THE INSTRUMENTS

Despite the "defining" descriptions above, just about every possible configuration of flogging instrument is available (homemade or store-bought) in nearly infinite variants. Some of the differences matter very much to some of the players.

Length and weight are properties of an instrument which need to be right for the Top. One rule of thumb about length is that floggers and cats, including the handle, but not including any tags ("fringe") at the ends of the tails, should be no longer than the Top's arm, measured from the shoulder seam of a T-shirt to the fingertips. As is the case with all rules of thumb, people develop their own version of the rule. Many men prefer two or three more inches overall length, while a lot of women are forced by the scarcity of good whips in short lengths to learn to use instruments longer than their comfort really dictates.

Weight is definitely a comfort issue. Some Tops don't mind a whip that feels heavy in their hands, although that will mean having to put more energy into swinging it. Other Tops, possibly the majority, prefer a whip to be light enough that it carries itself almost effortlessly once it is in motion, so they spend less energy per stroke while using that instrument.

Most Tops find that the length they come to think of ideal for themselves is the same for all weights and styles of floggers and cats. And, again, *most* Tops find that they are more willing to accept potentially uncomfortable weight (either too light or too heavy) in an instrument that is to be used more sparingly: a heavy cat intended to be used only at the ends of scenes, for instance, or a very light warm-up instrument (nylon or silk-thread tails) that will be toyed with or used briefly at the start of a scene.

Balance is surely the most talked-about and probably the least understood feature of floggers and cats. The rule of thumb here is that the instrument, gripped

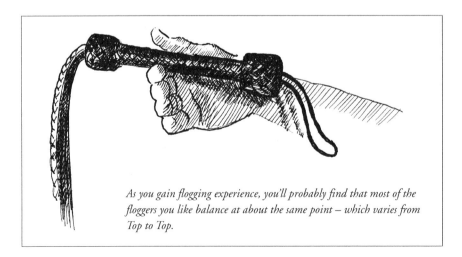

As you gain flogging experience, you'll probably find that most of the floggers you like balance at about the same point – which varies from Top to Top.

comfortably on the handle (not the knot at the end of the handle), then released to rest on the forward (index) finger of the grip, should balance there. The handle, to do this, has to be weighted to match the weight of the tails plus the weight of the forward inches of the handle. In fact, if comfort is the issue, the most perfect balance for most Tops is about an inch forward from the index finger in this grip test. And, to be perfectly blunt, the balance that will be comfortable for a given Top should be discovered personally and over a long period of time. Nonetheless, this test will at least give you a starting point in determining what works for you.

To discover what balance you like, do lots of flogging, then set aside the one or two floggers and the one or two cats you find yourself most comfortable with. Try the grip test, repeating and adjusting it until you find where these favorite instruments balance on your finger. Chances are that you will discover they all balance at about the same point in relation to your relaxed grip – the balance point may be at the index finger, inside the closed hand, one or more inches forward from the index finger… or wherever. If you discover that your favorite whips do not have any common factor among them with regard to where their balance point is, then you are a Top whose style, strength, energy reserves, etc. make balance a non-issue. Don't think about it.

All the same, extremely out-of-balance floggers do exist. Massive quantities of oil-tanned leather tails, for instance, will outweigh any reasonable handle they can be attached to. For a few minutes on the right occasion, this is fine. For a big enough and strong enough Top, it may also be fine. But, for most Tops or for extended use, these tail-heavy floggers will be exhausting because, as the tails are not counterbalanced by the handle, all the lifting and swinging is being done by muscle power. A balanced whip benefits a good deal more from the physics of centrifugal motion.

Until now, the question of balance has been discussed as though the only possible problem were too much tail weight for too little handle weight. The opposite does happen. This is usually less of an issue because they instruments in question are specialty items anyway, and seldom used for long. With an instrument that is handle-heavy, the centrifugal drag of the tails in the air can be exhausting and uncomfortable when the whip is used in heavy strokes (which is unlikely).

The materials from which flogging instruments can be made vary tremendously. Leather obviously predominates, but rubber and vinyl and neoprene and nylon, silk and cotton, chain and wire, Teflon and hemp are all seen fairly often, and new materials are being tried out all the time. The first thing to consider when looking at a non-leather instrument is how it will feel, what sensation it will produce. There is no better way to answer this question than to give yourself several good whacks. As a back-up, for the Top too timid to take even a scrap of what she gives out in abundance, an experienced bottom who is well-known to the Top can be called on to taste the instrument and report. The only wrong way to go is to just grab the instrument and start using it in a scene. The possible surprises are not all guaranteed to be welcome.

With so many materials available, it would be impossible to include details on all of them in a book. Besides, any attempt to do so would ensure that the book would be out-of-date before it could be published. So, if you are unfamiliar with the material, you should find out – from the whip maker if possible – about the cleaning and care of the material before buying and using it. You should also see if there are definite do's and don'ts as to how the material is safely stored. Finally, unless it is very obvious, check how the whip maker believes the material will stand up to blood and other body fluids and the cleaning required to remove them.

Choose your implements to fit your scene. An interrogation scene is no place for a frat paddle.

Chain-tailed floggers, for example, have to be kept very dry in storage, while it is possible, on the other hand, to keep leather and vinyl floggers too dry. Some space-age materials like Teflon resist damage from being crumpled up in a box because they are, as it is said, "high-integrity" materials, while others will "remember" any curve or bend you give them in storage.

Just as you must learn to *use* new instruments, you have to find ways to discover the other information you need to *maintain* them properly.

Fantasy value can matter, too. A horse fancier who does flogging, Top or bottom, may find quirts and crops especially exciting or completely ridiculous. A fantasy involving a pirate and his captive(s) might be destroyed by the introduction of a Neoprene flogger and greatly enhanced by the use of a cat made by unlaying and rebraiding a piece of rigging rope. This is usually not a major factor, but it is something you will want to consider when choosing instruments for some fantasy-based scenes.

Strokes or "Throws" of the Instruments

Variety is the spice of SM and uniqueness is often the hallmark of experience, but everyone needs some starting points. The strokes described below are basics of a sort. They are not detailed "to death" because you will make your own variations which you will either fall into on your own, or learn from your favorite whips. You will also learn from others by watching and imitating them as well as by actually asking for assistance or attending a demonstration and class.

The X or figure-8 is the most common stroke, and the most easily mastered as well. To learn it, pick up your flogger, bend your arm at the elbow so that your upper arm is more or less straight up and down, and swing the flogger with your forearm and wrist so that the tails draw a figure-8 lying on its side in the air.

The basic figure-8 stroke is versatile and relatively easy to learn.

As soon as the figure-8 is consistent, being drawn evenly and the same on every pass, step up to a wall or the back of a tall chair until the tails are brushing against it. Notice where in the figure-8 motion the touching takes place. For most Tops, the most effective version of the figure-8 stroke is done by having the tails land on the inner sides of the upper half of the lazy-8. More precisely, if the two circles are seen as clocks, most Tops tend to like having the tails touch down between the 12 and the 3 on the left clock-face and between the 12 and the 9 on the right clock-face. If your stroke is not doing this – if it is, for example, landing at the cross-point between the two halves of the 8 – decide for yourself if that is OK. It probably is not. Then, work on it until you are able to choose where on the figure-8 the tails will be touching the wall, chair or, eventually, the bottom. All possible contact choices will have their place in a well-developed arsenal of flogging skills.

If your arm position changes radically from the forearm-up-and-down position you were told to start in, again, it is your choice whether this works for you. Most Tops find it tiring to have the upper arm extended very much of the time.

With your upper arm pretty much in line with your body, you have a lot of latitude about how the strokes land. A broader stroke, where more inches of the tails will land together on the target, is created by pushing the forearm forward just slightly. This will be, of course, a more-thud stoke, and a harder one unless you compensate by also slowing down the motion of the whip. A tighter area can be struck, leaving only the very tips of the tails to land, by just pulling the upper arm back an inch or two. If this pull-back is done late enough and fast enough, you can create a snapping stroke which will be very high-sting and "authoritative."

The free-fall or paintbrush stroke is less common but adds a lower-level or lighter touch to your options. To learn this one, start out positioned as you were for the figure-8. Instead of drawing any figure in the air, experiment with ways of tossing the tails up, easing your arm forward an inch of two, and letting the tails fall. It is relatively easy to learn to drop the tails where you want them to land. Try that a few times before adding anything further. You will see that the stroke tends to be loose, the tails not tightly gathered. This is part of what makes the stroke so light.

When you are ready for a variation, try snapping the tails back with your wrist just as they land. This will gather them together, increase the intensity of the sensation delivered, and still be a relatively light stroke. It may take a while to learn to put this snap into the landing point of the stroke without pulling the tails completely off the bottom. Along the way, if you overdo the snap of the wrist, you'll whack yourself on every throw – probably in the crotch or on the thigh – but you'll survive it.

Horizontal plane strokes are very useful, easily learned and can be applied with excellent control and accuracy by even novice Tops. They are, basically, just what the name implies: strokes in which the line drawn in the air by the moving tails is parallel with the floor. There can be many variants on this general style, but

The horizontal stroke can be applied either with the Top facing the bottom (shown here), or to the bottom's side.

two are common and learning the two will give you everything you need to develop your own versions.

The simplest horizontal plane stroke is done just by swinging the flogger back and forth in front of yourself. It is best to start in the same upper-arm-down position as for the earlier strokes. Do not let yourself fall into the easy trap of swinging your whole body right and left. Instead, make the motion with your forearm and wrist – more wrist this time than with the earlier strokes. Notice how the tails gather more when you move the whip faster, so that faster motion means a smaller, more controlled area of contact. Notice that you can add a snap to this stroke by a sudden increase in the speed just before it brushes the wall or bottom.

When done correctly, with sufficient follow-through, the fall or end of the stroke will usually be at the Top's side or back. That is, you *will* be hitting yourself with this stroke. However, if you stop pushing the whip as soon as it makes contact with the bottom, your body will just be the object against which a slow-moving clump of leather stops. You will not be giving yourself a pain-trip... unless you choose to do so.

The second version of the horizontal plane stroke is the one Dennis used with mark, like a baseball player at bat. It can't be described any better than that. Turn your side to the pitcher (bottom!) and swing. After a few practice strokes on

The vertical stroke is intuitive to most Tops. Care must be taken to land the tails on muscle, not on the tops of the shoulders or the slope of the upper buttocks.

something inanimate, you're ready to go, but realize this is not a good stroke early in most scenes, and many bottoms are never ready for it. Also, such heavily landed strokes can easily knock an unrestrained bottom off his feet.

Vertical plane strokes are also useful, particularly in small space, but they can hardly make an overly restricted space really useful for flogging. Vertical plane strokes are, as the name implies, throws that move straight up and down, or nearly so. These are usually used very lightly during warm-up or very heavily late in the scene. The version of the vertical stroke most frequently seen is done by bending the arm up so that the hand is near the shoulder, with the handle of the flogger more or less pointing at the bottom and the tails hanging down behind the Top. With a swift lift and forward swing, the tails are brought down on the bottom's back or butt, and the stroke ends with the flogger hanging to the floor, the Top's arm extended straight down.

These throws are not rhythmically repeating ones, but independent actions. You have to, in effect, reload between shots – get the flogger positioned again. During early warm-up, they can be used as fanning strokes and grazing strokes to help your eye-hand coordination reset for the scene, giving you a clear, well-imprinted measure of the distance to the bottom. Later, used heavily, they can be jolting body blows. In either application, there is a danger of the vertical plane stroke wrapping over the bottom's shoulders and allowing the ends of the flogger tails to literally crack into the "unsuspecting" chest or collar bone. You will want to practice until you are sure you can avoid this happening.

Circular strokes are usually what a completely inexperienced person does the first time he or she picks up a flogger. They spin the tails in a circle, like the propeller on small airplane. If the hand is turned out, the circle is beside the Top and can be directed to the target while the Top is facing the bottom's back. With the hand in a more relaxed position at the front of the Top's body, the circle is created on a plane in front of him, so that he must turn side-on to the bottom to deliver the stroke. Either way, this stroke should not be permitted to be more than a rare variation in your style. First, simple as it is, it turns out to be hard to control. Second, it never develops much from the simplicity of its native form, so it begins to feel and look jejune as the rest of your flogging develops. And, finally – perhaps most importantly – this stroke is very hard on your floggers. The twisting and tight rubbing of the tails right at the point where they meet the handle can become very intense. This is already the point at which floggers are most likely to wear out. The wear is multiplied tremendously by a circular stroke which, in any case, is an unattractive and not-terribly-useful throw.

Overhead strokes can be pictured pretty well from the description of Dennis using them: the flogger is swung around like a helicopter's main rotor *overhead*. The swinging around part of the stroke is very easily mastered, of course. The art in the stroke – and this one requires some art to work effectively – comes in being able to tip the "rotor" down for contact with the bottom without tipping in too far and with some degree of accuracy in terms of where it strikes. This comes very naturally for some people and is next to impossible for others, but it can be learned by everyone.

It is wise to practice the overhead circular stroke first in the direction you "naturally" start swinging the flogger, then to also learn to be equally accurate with the whip moving in the opposite direction. The reason to make this throw bi-directional is simply that moving into and out of overhead strokes from any other stroke is easier, more fluid and less of an interruption of the rhythm you are working with if you can just lift the flogger and keep striking.

Overhead strokes can be brutally heavy because you have, in addition to the energy you put into the throw, all the advantage of coming from above – which means that gravity is on your side.

Notice that the overhead stroke is unlike the previously mentioned circular stroke. In the overhead stroke, you do not allow the tails to travel in a circle while the flogger handle remains fixed. Instead, you create the overhead circle with arm motion, swinging your entire arm in the full circle, so the tails maintain their regular relationship with the handle.

This can be a very dramatic throw, but remember how much space you are consuming behind yourself. Suddenly switching to an overhead stroke can be effective and interesting, but it can be a great surprise to a bystander behind you. Also, since you are using your whole arm for this stroke, you will probably find that you need to step back slightly to land the strokes well. This split second in which you move a few inches back from the bottom can also give you a chance to be sure no one is standing too near behind you.

The wet-towel stroke is easy to do and just as easy to screw up. People often use this stroke with single-tailed whips, but usually only when they are new to the single-tail or when they are "playing around." To do this stroke, hold the flogger in your dominant hand and lift up near or past the opposite shoulder; gather the tails in your other hand and aim at the bottom – pretty much as if you were about to shoot a rubber band at her. Let the hand on the flogger tails provide some resistance as you push forward with the flogger handle in a sudden and uninterrupted movement. The tails zing outward toward the bottom only to be suddenly stopped and "cracked" just as you would with a wet towel. The result is an increase in the whip's sting quotient beyond all expectation, and a throw that can be very accurate with little practice. This is not a shot you will want to use a great deal, but it is a useful one in many instances. Since the whip remains always between the Top and bottom, as with the vertical plane strokes, this is a throw that can be accommodated in relatively restricted space.

When you want time to judge the state of the bottom, this is a good stroke to fill-in with. It keeps the scene going, and continues the stimulation of the bottom It keeps you active and involved, But it can be done slowly enough – strokes spaced as you choose – to allow you real time to check in visually and get a good idea of the bottom's responses and condition.

Cooling strokes are sometimes called for. What "cooling stroke" means is any contact you make with the bottom's skin, using a flogger or other instrument, which is aimed at spacing the impact blows or soothing the leathered-up area or providing some kind of stimulation between actual blows. In a long flogging scene, it is sometimes useful to resort to cooling strokes a number of times. They give the Top a chance to get a close look at the bottom to judge her state and to give his own arm a little break as well.

Some people perform this "cooling" by dangling the flogger in the air above the bottom's back and brushing or tickling the back by jiggling or swinging the tails of the flogger. Others hold the flogger against their own bodies, usually above waist level, and use their other hand to hold the flogger tails together, making a short brush-like bundle of the tips of the tails to "dust" the flogged area. Of course, the same effect can be achieved with kisses, licking, grazing the area gently with beard, the Top's hair or another flogging instrument. An available pervertible such as a nylon-net dish scrubber or a handful of facial tissues will also so nicely.

It is not unheard of for a Top to replace the cooling strokes, when she feels they are needed, with some other kind of activity altogether, like rolling a cool orange over the hot skin or "shaving" the area with the edge of an ice cube. If the Top has a bottle of water at hand, some of the water could be dribbled from the bottle or the Top's mouth onto the hot, flogged skin.

The idea with cooling strokes is largely to extend the flogging. They connect Top and bottom in a way that is otherwise usually lost during a longer flogging, and they turn down the heat, literally, so the action can continue at a higher level for a longer time overall.

READING THE BOTTOM

Even the most stoic and inexpressive bottom gives some signals that an observant Top can read. Maybe it would be interesting if all bottoms gave some visible and intentional indication of how they are being affected by the flogging in progress, but sometimes you get only the biological signs. What's more, the biological signs vary a good deal from person to person. So, to some extent, reading the bottom is akin to the mind-reading a lot of bottoms apparently expect of their Tops.

Skin is the obvious starting point in any discussion about "reading" a bottom's reaction to flogging. Skin response and other biological cues are also the only absolutely, positively honest feedback you can count on. A bottom may lie, misreport or mistake his own reactions in any number of ways with any number of conscious or unconscious motives, but the story displayed on the skin is genuine. Sadly, not all bodies have identical responses to flogging. Some can be quite surprising, so nothing replaces experience with the body in question. But there are some generalities that are very nearly universal.

In the beginning, during the warm-up phase of the flogging, the first strokes should be light enough to make no mark. If the earliest strokes leave marks, you may want to check yourself; it is possible to start too fast. Besides, the no trace of contact phase only runs for seconds or, at most, a few minutes. This stage of the flogging is basically just communicating to the bottom where the flogging will be and giving both partners a chance to "get there" for the scene. (Obviously, saying the strokes "should be" anything sounds more forceful than it would ideally be. Do what you do, what works for you and for your partner. These are generalities based on some experience, but they do not take into account *your* experience or your style.)

During this phase you are also imprinting yourself – the Top – with the geography of the scene space. If this is done effectively, and even consciously, the result will be that you can move around a good deal and still always automatically sense or correctly judge the distance to the target area.

The Top will know when the warm-up has been sufficient by reading the bottom – not by looking at the clock. While warm-up can usually be quite brief – since the flogging will then build up slowly, seducing consent and consuming being in a sense a matter of never going faster or further than the current level of warming-up permits – some bottoms require special attention in this phase. Whether the reasons are physical, meaning they are connected to pain tolerance, or they are psychological, the flogging should be kept painless and leave no marks until the bottom is ready and the Top is sure of this fact.

After the area is defined by no-mark strokes and the bottom is ready to move on, the whip can land more heavily and leave stripes. Done carefully, these stripes will only very gradually increase in coloring and will cover the entire area to be flogged before the next stage is attempted. As the stripes left by individual strokes of the flogger tails reach a point of having hatch-marked the entire area you intend to flog, it should be possible to increase the energy you are putting into each stroke. At this point you should begin to see that where the lines intersect or overlap, they leave a more intense color – usually redder, with the earlier lines being more pink by comparison.

If you continue to work with increasingly energetic strokes (or move to a heavier flogger), the next change in the skin's report should be a generalizing of the redness. Peter Fiske, a highly respected leatherman and whip collector in San Francisco, calls this generalizing of the skin color "leathering up," and the term is distinctly appropriate. What the skin is reporting is that the body is now checking out the site of the flogging, determining whether the body is experiencing a trauma that requires attention. Fluids, including blood (which provides the color), are pumped into the area. This causes a slight puffiness or swelling which, in effect, connects all the dots and lines and raises the skin of the whole affected area. If you were to stop right here, the leathering up would subside very quickly, probably leaving no trace, but it would be a rough few minutes for the bottom because the body's question about whether the site needed attention would be unanswered and the body chemistry involved would be confused and confusing.

If you continue, the next stage in skin response is a tightening of the leathered-up area. The skin sometimes shifts color to a deeper red at this point, but sometimes the color shift just doesn't occur. What must happen is that the skin tightens from the increase of fluids just beneath the surface. This often gives the skin, seen from very close, a kind of orange-peel appearance in which every pore is visible. By now the skin is also hot to the touch from the blood rushing through so near the surface. This is all good. The reason the body is fluid-filling the area is to increase blood flow enough to carry the famous endorphins and opioids to the site. These naturally occurring pain-control "drugs" are essential to the bottom's experience, just as they are to our management of all pain and bodily trauma. In sufficient quantities, encouraged over a long enough time, these natural drugs can produce a genuine "high" like the one long-distance runners and other high-exertion athletes speak of. (For an interesting discussion of opioids and endorphins, see *Urban Aboriginals* by Geoff Mains.) The body also brings clotting factors and other chemistry into the neighborhood in case they are needed to deal with the "trauma."

When the skin is leathered up (generally puffed up), tightened and hot to the touch, the warm-up is complete. On this basis, a flogging as intense as the bottom can bear may now proceed. The area is both desensitized to the unpleasant kind of pain reaction because of the pain-killing effects of the blood chemistry, and hypersensitized to stimulation in general because of the biological attention the area is getting from inside. What's more, the bottom is now psychologically prepared, because the same blood chemistry that is reaching the back or butt or thighs is also washing through the brain. And, on a more mundane level, the bottom has probably been allowed to reconfirm the trust needed for the scene.

Later stages of the flogging, as read in the skin, are primarily communications about what the aftereffects of the scene will be. Bruising, for instance, will become obvious, breaks in the skin and bleeding may be seen, and these can be understood as fair indicators of what will remain of the flogging the next day. It should be understood, though, that the degree of bruising can be very deceptive and that breaks in the skin and bleeding will both be more intense during and immediately following the scene than later.

Bruising occurs when blood becomes trapped in or just under the skin. Depending on the bottom's health and physical condition, this trapped blood – from damaged capillaries and other non-emergency trauma – may be carried away very quickly in the hours following the scene. Other bottoms respond in what is, in visual terms, the opposite way. The bruising seems slight during the scene, but increases later as more blood becomes trapped or the coloration of the skin fades to reveal the bruises. Experience will teach you to recognize the physical types and the signs of health and conditioning that result in each of these "miscommunications" about bruising, but you will always be open to surprises when flogging a bottom with whom you are unfamiliar.

Breaks in the skin, often cuts from the edges of flogger tails on tightly leathered-up skin, always seem worse during than after a flogging. The reasons for this are relatively easy to understand. The tight, swollen skin is stretched over a larger mass, ballooned out, if you will, so it effectively pulls the cut open. As the swelling subsides, the smallest breaks close up completely and the edges of more severe cuts relax back into alignment with one another as well.

Bleeding is also more intense while the body is super-supplying the area with blood. When there is no more "traumatic" stimulation being supplied, the blood flow returns to normal levels pretty quickly in most bodies and the bleeding subsides or stops. Of course, it is also difficult for blood to clot while the area is being beaten and the fluid presence is great. It is also unlikely that clotted blood will remain where it clots, instead it will be wiped away by the next flogger stroke. So, again, the natural tendency of the body to prevent blood loss will not be in full effect until after the flogging stops.

There is one other effect to be read from the skin: weeping. The phenomenon called "weeping" occurs when plasma, the colorless liquid part of blood, oozes through the skin. This usually happens in fully leathered-up skin before any bruising or bleeding begins, but the variations are so extreme that it is nearly meaningless with a bottom you have not flogged before. Some people's skin weeps as soon as the skin begins to swell; for others (most?) the weeping is an indication that the swelling has reached its limit. This is a "reading" to which you will only be able to assign meaning when you know the bottom's body from repeated previous floggings, but it is a sign you will not want to ignore. You will see it as a sweat-like wetness of the skin which is stickier than sweat, doesn't run or evaporate easily and, if tasted, is not as salty. Of course, tasting plasma *is* a transfer of bodily fluids and, while probably harmless, it may be beyond your own safer sex limits.

Muscles also send signals which can be very honest or, rarely, not at all honest. Trust the signs read in the muscles as you would trust the bottom in question, no more and no less. You might even ask a bottom whose muscular reactions you suspect are being exaggerated to relax and let you see the unedited version of the bodily responses. The messages from muscles come in three time-based categories: early reactions, conscious reactions and involuntary reactions.

Early in a flogging, the muscles should react very little. If you do the warm-up at a pace that is right for that bottom at that time under those conditions, the "correct" muscular response, in fact, will be relaxation. With careful timing and predictable rhythms, this effect can be maintained, turning a flogging into a massage. To do so, you simply maintain the highest level of stimulation that gets no reactive response other than relaxation and flattening or smoothing from the muscles. If you are a careful muscle-reader, this can go on for hours and result in a relatively intense (never extreme or brutal) flogging. It can also be very exhausting for the Top to continue exercising this level of whip control for the long time involved.

Assuming you are not trying to produce a massage, but intend to give a genuine flogging including manageable pain, the early stages of the muscle response will still be relaxation. If there are twitches or flinches during warm-up, you are possibly moving too quickly, allowing the strokes to become more intense than you have prepared to skin and muscle to accept. If you see anything beyond the mildest flinch, often followed by the bottom intentionally moving or shaking the body part or muscle, consider decreasing the intensity of the stroke to a point where you get no muscle reaction before the skin begins to leather up. "Consider" is consider... you will know by the atmosphere between yourself and the bottom whether to push ahead or let up a bit, and it is often entirely acceptable to push ahead, especially if a relatively intense scene is intended.

After the skin is leathered up, the muscles – increasingly showered in endorphins as you go along – respond very differently. The reactions here are the ones we are calling "conscious," although that term is more a convenience than a description.

Because the body is conducting its research about the nature of the trauma and the biochemical needs of the area, muscles will sometimes suddenly clench then slowly relax. This is a sign that all is well. So long as every muscle that flexes also smooths out fairly quickly, the body is handling the level of stimulation perfectly. If muscles, even one muscle, clenches and does not soon relax, there is a high likelihood that the bottom is having trouble processing the pain, and you might want to ease up or at least slow down the acceleration of intensity. Obviously, a muscle that flexes and remains flexed for very long will cramp. You don't want to be the cause of this kind of scene-endangering discomfort while you are trying to hurt the bottom in a different, altogether more manageable way. It may be necessary to stop for a moment and manually massage a cramped muscle. This can be done without breaking the scene dynamic so long as the verbal exchange, if any, is kept scene-specific.

These muscle responses are conscious only in that the bottom is aware of them. It is not that the bottom chooses or directs them. This is the area where the bottom who is trying too hard to communicate with the Top will make mistakes that often have to be understood as false reports. It is fine for the bottom to be aware of these muscular reactions. It creates no problem if the bottom participates in relaxing the tensed muscle. But, for want of a clearer word, some bottoms start lying at this stage by intentionally flexing and relaxing muscles. This only serves to confuse the genuine bodily responses and should be discouraged as strongly as possible. Any such wakeful and controlled muscle reactions must be seen as such and understood as "verbal" communications, which are discussed in the following sectcion.

In the later stages of a flogging that becomes sufficiently intense or effective, the muscles sometimes begin to react in ways that are completely involuntary. The bottom may or may not even be able to register the fact that these responses are happening, and the bottom's apparent awareness or ignorance of them is part of what you want to read.

Involuntary muscular reactions can be anything from a single muscle quivering to the whole body moving or shaking in either a coordinated or a completely uncoordinated fashion. So, at this stage, there are three categories of information being communicated by the muscles. We might say that the movement is the language or the message itself, the degree to which the bottom is aware of these movements is the tone or urgency in the communication, and the level of coordination is the accent which tells us, in a sense, how "far away" the bottom is.

The language of involuntary muscle reactions is always a foreign language to a novice and differs from bottom to bottom so that, in a way, it is always foreign enough to require translation, at least until the two partners in the flogging are very familiar with each other. The "words" and word-order are extremely individual but, thankfully, they tend to remain the same with the same bottom in the same state time after time. Common "phrases" include slow-motion swaying or ultra-slow-motion stomping of one foot, nodding or even relatively violent shaking of the head, whole-body quivering or trembling, and an apparently voluntary but wild rattling or shaking of the dungeon equipment or restraints. The involuntary communication is usually fairly continuous once it begins and can be frightening in its intensity. Properly understood, however, it guides the scene forward.

Coordinated muscle movements like the ones described in the previous paragraph are almost always statements that include "all is well" in them, but they also suggest that you have reached at least the neighborhood of the bottom's pain-tolerance limits. If you are able to maintain the coordinated nature of the movements by staying at the level of stimulation already achieved or pulling back slightly, the scene may go on for some time. If the movements become *uncoordinated*, you are losing the bottom, getting too close to or surpassing limits. Be careful here. One step past the actual limits, you are – at least in the later assessment of the bottom – probably being abusive or becoming one of those miserable Tops of whom it is said that he can't take no for an answer. You will know that you are working the situation correctly if you can guide the involuntary muscle response up and down slightly in intensity by adjusting the intensity of your stimulation. The less you are able to influence the muscle reactions, the closer the scene has come to the bottom's final limitations. And, on the other hand, pushing forward even rapidly at this point is sometimes what the bottom wants. Go figure!

To get a grasp of a particular bottom's involuntary language of muscle reactions, you will need a good deal of experience with that person. Some generalities are possible. If the movement remains coordinated and at normal speed, especially if it involves only large muscles such as the glutes and the upper leg muscles, you are still in "safe" territory, *probably*. The further from this the reaction goes, the less sure you can be that you are still on the right side of the bottom's limits. That is, if the movements start out coordinated but become uncoordinated, if they involve smaller muscles such as the neck, the calves or the muscles covering the ribs, or if the reaction starts out at normal speed but suddenly revs up or closes down to slow-motion, these things suggest a much closer brush with the final limits of the bottom. On the other hand, if the movements start out super-slow or very fast, if their first manifestation is in the smaller muscles or if they were conflicted and uncoordinated to begin with, you just have a more "foreign" language to contend with.

The muscles of the hands and face are not to be taken as small muscles in this sense. They are discussed as "verbal" communications below. The muscles of the feet may either be considered small muscles or verbal communicators, depending on the bottom in question. It is not uncommon for a bottom, for example, to pull up to tiptoe as an intentional – verbal – communication. However, if you ask the bottom to put his feet flat on the floor, and he is surprised to find himself on tiptoe, you have just discovered that this was truly a non-verbal communication.

The bottom's awareness or unawareness of these muscle reactions provide the tone of urgency or relative triviality the Top must also understand. Of course, you can not ask if the bottom knows what she is doing in most cases. That would break the spell you have spent so much energy creating. By being alert to the bodily response *to* the involuntary reaction, however, you will know with some degree of certainty whether the bottom is aware of and able to influence the movement. This is tone only. In effect, it tells you whether to read the muscle movement as screaming and humming. If the bottom has no discernible awareness of the muscle movements, the body is screaming, but it is not necessarily screaming "stop!" If terror is sexy for the bottom (and the Top), or if it is intended that the bottom's limits should be challenged, this screaming tone may be perfectly acceptable. If the bottom is either adding to the reaction or otherwise apparently responding to it – even trying to resist it – the tone is one of humming, and all is well if you can keep it just that way. As long as the tone is in this lower register, the bottom's actual limits are not being breached, although he may be going further than he has gone before.

The coordination of these muscle reactions, or their lack of coordination, is an entirely involuntary indicator of how far from "ordinary consciousness" the bottom has traveled in the flogging. Whether she is able to intentionally resist or influence the movements or not, the bottom's body will maintain a degree of coordination in the movements until the mental state "goes away" to a point where the "ground" is unfamiliar. While this discussion borders on the spiritual and certainly could benefit from the language of psychological professionals, we don't need to invoke either God or Freud to understand it.

A fair indication of uncoordinated muscular activity is that the muscles either don't work together, meaning that, for example, the upper arm pulls while the lower arm quivers and freezes, or they actually create situations where one activity directly interferes with another as, for example, the flailing arms strike the waggling head. This occurs earlier for some bottoms, but usually happens when you have reached the bottom's limit in the ability to process (and bear) the stimulation being provided. How to react depends on what has been negotiated or what is intended, but to *ignore* the body language when this accent is introduced is seldom a good idea. Very commonly, a combination of skin-to-skin contact and a brief period with no new stimulation will bring the bottom back and give the body a chance to get coordinated. At that point, it may be time to cool down and stop the flogging, or it may be time to start working at a level below the one that inspired the uncoordinated reaction in order to continue. The difference, again, is what you are going for in the scene.

Verbal cues can be important, but they are the least reliable in terms of honest representation of actual experience. Bottoms will even tell Tops after a scene sometimes that they wish they had not been taken seriously when they said "stop" or whatever. On the other hand, not listening to the verbal cues can lead to the accusation that you have failed to take practice safe, sane, consensual SM; that you have become abusive; that you can not be trusted as a Top. Your own reading, depending on the bottom and the situation, will have to tell you whether to trust the bottom's words or not; often, you will find the best path is to act as if you believed and trusted the bottom's words. Later, this decision can become central to the negotiation of a more intense scene if that is what you both want.

One very good reason for a Top and a bottom to have agreed upon safewords in advance is to give the bottom the freedom to shout out anything, including "stop" or "you're killing me" or "don't hit me again," without disturbing the scene. The Top with a safeword in place can fairly safely ignore the actual words in any communication except the safeword itself. The sound of terror and panic, and the *appearance* of non-consensuality permitted when a bottom can say anything she wants without stopping or destroying the scene, are essential for some players.

Frankly, bottoms can learn to either speak honestly during a scene or to accept the consequences of not doing so, but everyone is safer if they learn this by *not* being pushed beyond what they say. The opposite track, giving them what you suppose they want regardless of what they say, is fraught with just too many dangers, most of them damaging to the Top's access to other bottoms in the future. Again, with a safeword in place, the bottom can even be encouraged to say what makes him feel good and what supports his own fantasies about being flogged. Until the Top hears the agreed-upon safeword, he continues, following other signals like tone and the messages from the body, but ignoring the "stop" words that are other than the safeword.

The physical facts about the body which are most powerfully controlled by the conscious mind are those concerning the small muscles: face and hands, mostly. These muscles are constantly used in verbal communications outside SM, and the fact that a flogging is in progress is unlikely to change the usual use of face and hand muscles. Grimaces and fists, smiles and relaxed hands, leers and fingers scratching idly at the air should all be taken to mean during a flogging pretty much what they mean at any other time. They are a few degrees more automatic than words and, therefore, a few degrees more reliable as indicators of the bottom's current experience. Contradictory combinations of facial expressions and words can be very confusing such as when the bottom has a beatific smile and is saying "I can't take any more." Only familiarity or "instinct" will clarify the disconsonance, but it is usually advisable to go with the words if you hope to have the same bottom back another time.

Often, you can just point out the contradiction and get a verbal correction from the bottom. "You're smiling and saying 'don't," you might say, "so is it good or is it stop?" The bottom will now give you an answer you can safely trust because he is being drawn to and made attentive to the consequences of the next thing he says. Even so, you cannot assume that a bottom who urges you to trust a facial expression one time will thank you for ignoring words the next time.

Nonverbal sounds are also important. Sounds that are wordless are usually produced with less artifice or conscious invention than words, just as hand gestures and facial expressions are. Purring and growling, whimpering and crying, guttural howls and constrained squeaks all tend to be encouragement to the Top. The only kind of nonverbal sound that should really give a Top reason to consider that she may be pushing too hard is the sound of panic in any form – impossible to describe and equally impossible to miss when you hear it. Generally, you can be guided by the nonverbal sounds in a thermostat-like fashion. You will hear the sounds that indicate real pleasure or satisfaction and the ones that tend to suggest discomfort or the approach of panic. Then the trick is to play as hard as you can in the former register without invoking any sounds from the latter.

Bottoms who know they are likely to shout a good deal should tell the Top in advance. As part of the negotiations, a very noisy bottom, or one who knows he screams like he's dying when he's fine, should just explain the situation. A gag may be needed, and the Top may require the bottom to supply some details as to what kinds of words or noises he should understand as "bad."

Also, bottoms who know that other things – like crying or becoming silent – indicate the end of the scene for them should definitely share this information with the Top. If the Top doesn't know for sure whether crying, for example, means that the scene has ended for the bottom, he may continue, thinking that to keep the crying going is a welcome effect, perhaps even a much-wanted catharsis.

Hands in particular should be watched during a flogging. The reason for this is twofold. One, the use of the hands is beautifully positioned on the conscious-subconscious border line, so they will often "speak" somewhat honestly and earlier than other signals. If you're watching them closely enough, you'll even catch the mental editing of hand postures and learn how and when to trust them. And, two, the hands are often also reacting to some extent to the bondage or the restraints. During a flogging, it is wise to be sure the bondage or restraints remain as they were installed, not twisted or tightened or otherwise changed. The first indication that a restraint has become twisted or too tight will be in the hand or hands affected. So, an incomprehensible gesture may be about the flogging or just about the restraint. It's worth checking.

A NOTE ON SINGLE-TAILED WHIPS

While it may not be generally accepted that the word "flog" includes the use of single-tailed whips, the reality is that many people these days include a signal whip or other short, single-tailed whip in the scene along with their floggers and cats. The skills involved in the use of single-tailed whips can be quite different from those required to use floggers and cats. Separate single-tail classes are regularly taught at leatherfests and club events. It is possible to use a short single-tail in a flogger-like way, though. If you do this, the whip will eventually give you the schooling you need to use it more proficiently. And, if you come to the conclusion that you have a taste for using single-tails, you can take one of those special classes, too.

To make use of a single-tail in a flogging scene, you will want to remove the cracker or see that it is quite short. If you don't do this, you will run into control problems that are the specific domain of the single-tail and not covered in a text about flogging. You will want the whip to be quite short as well, probably 42 inches or less, although a big enough Top may find the system described below workable with a whip of up to 48 inches.

Single-tail whips are dangerous. So are many of the tools we use to provide mutually satisfying SM experiences for ourselves and our partners. However, the single-tail can be used safely and effectively if you forget about its ability to crack. Think of that, for now, as either a rodeo art or something, in any case, for another time. Most people attempt to learn to use single-tail whips by cracking them, but it is not frequently an appropriate approach for SM players who have not had personal training in that use of the whip. What follows here is an outline developed and very successfully used to teach flogging Tops how to employ single tails:

- *First series of steps:* 1) Own your own short whip, 32 to 48 inches long, preferably shorter rather than longer to begin with. 2) Practice swinging the whip accurately in a level plane, a tilted plane, etc., but without cracking it. 3) Practice drawing a line across a target (such as a pillow) until you are able to "draw" accurately. 4) Practice drawing

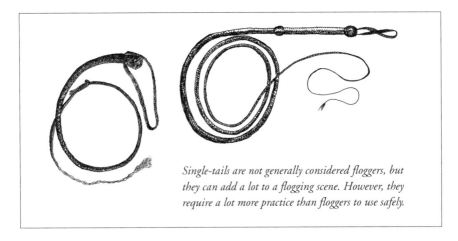

Single-tails are not generally considered floggers, but they can add a lot to a flogging scene. However, they require a lot more practice than floggers to use safely.

your line more and more rapidly without losing your accuracy. 5) Practice drawing your line rapidly while changing the plane of the stroke, back and forth between level, horizontal strokes and any angle you find comfortable, without losing your accuracy. At this stage you almost surely will begin to draw lazy-8 figures as well as lines. This is fine; do what feels good. 6) As you encounter moves that don't fall well after contact with the target, work at correcting those falls or follow-throughs. When you are comfortable with your ability to draw lines at different angles in the air or on a pillow, move on to the second series of steps.

- *Second series of steps:* 1) Now that you have an idea of the action of the whip and the control of its follow-through, adjust your practice to *pull* the whip into its fall or follow-through. That is, as the whip makes contact, put a little added energy into drawing the instrument into the ending of the stroke. 2) Practice this adjustment repeatedly with the various planes of stroke direction. 3) Be sure to learn to recover (yes, you, the Top) from each stroke before starting the next. 4) Practice moving in and out by extending or withdrawing your arm and also by stepping or leaning slightly forward and back, so that you know when the stroke will hit the target, when not, and how hard it will land. 5) Also notice that you must land only the last few inches of the whip or only its shortened cracker. Now, move on to series three.

- *Third series of steps:* Now that you have control of the whip... don't laugh, you do have control of the whip at this point and it probably only took one or two hours' practice to get it... replace the pillow or now-streaked wall with a person who is willing to report on what you do with the whip. Repeat all the steps of the first two series using your drafted bottom as a target. Notice how your automatic caring for the fact that the target is human changes your relationship with the whip. This is to be expected. In fact, without that unexplainable shift in the Top's sense of the whip, this series of lessons would never work.

- *Final step:* Practice, practice, practice, but do it with a human target whenever possible, and always make yourself available to learn from those who are better, more experienced whip users, and accept their "system" of teaching and using the single-tail as much as you are able.

As for the cracking of the whip, you may learn it from the whip or not. You may learn it from another player or not. In the end, this non-cracking use of the single-tail is the use most appropriate to flogging in any case, although you may later wish to learn traditional, crack-to-use whip techniques as well.

SCENE THREE

DAWN AND LORI
FINALLY DO
A FLOGGING

Donna, KNOWN TO HER FRIENDS AS
Dawn, and Lori, known to everyone everywhere
as a pain-pig, have been looking forward to some
"quality play time" together for months. Dawn
has a vanilla lover who really doesn't want her
making SM dates unless they are separated by
circumstances, and she never wants to hear about
the "funny goings on," as she calls SM parties
and scenes. Lori is very single, but she's been
"previously engaged" every time Dawn has been
free. Finally, Dawn's lover is out of town on business for a couple of days and Lori is free!

The women met, as planned, for drinks
at a local men's bar where they knew they'd be
welcome if they came and went early enough.
By 9:30, they were at Lori's house, and somehow sex took over. After that, they slept, and
didn't wake again until nearly 1:00 AM, but they

were not going to let orgasms and napping get in the way of the flogging scene they had both been looking forward to.

Lori already had the space set up with a whipping bench, several of her floggers and paddles, and the ashtray and bottled water she knew Dawn would want. Lori preferred the bent-over and fully supported posture provided by the bench, and expected that Dawn would be ready to use whatever was available.

It seemed to Dawn that the scene went very well. She used every flogger that Lori had put out, left stripes all over Lori's back, butt and thighs, and got herself pretty worked up in the process. It was a scene like any flogging scene, except this one was with Lori, at last. Every time she'd given in and beaten one of her girlfriends, it had been the beginning of the end, but that would not happen this time, she was sure. This time she was with Lori, and everyone knew she could take it.

When Dawn was "over it," she put down the last whip, unshackled Lori, and helped her off the bench. "That was worth waiting for," she said. When Lori said nothing, Dawn added, "You OK?"

"No, I'm not," Lori answered. "Did you even know I was here, Dawn, or did you just think I was another layer of padding on that bench to make your whips sound good or something?"

"Hey, Lori, what's happening here?"

"Not SM," Lori answered, "that much I can tell you!"

With that, Lori turned and rushed into the bathroom, slamming the door behind her. Dawn just watched, wide-eyed and lost. She picked up her clothes and went to the half-bath by the front door where she washed up, dressed and stood there staring into the mirror for several minutes. When she came back to the bedroom, Lori was in bed, lying on a huge white towel with a blanket pulled up over her legs.

They alternately looked at each other and stared away into the air. After several tense minutes, Dawn walked over to the side of the bed. She felt Lori stiffen when she placed her hand on the red-welted shoulder. "Hurt?" she asked.

"Inside, outside, heart-side and every other way," Lori answered, sounding more bewildered than angry. After a moment, she pulled Dawn's hand off her shoulder and held it in both of her own hands against her chest. She took several deep breaths, obviously working through something she wanted to say, so Dawn didn't speak.

Finally, Lori started, "You don't even know... I can tell you don't, why would I ask? But... you don't know that this was... well, if this is a way to do SM, it is... anyway, not *my* way, not what I'm used to."

Slowly, understanding that her message might not be easy for Dawn to hear, Lori began composing her thoughts. And, just as slowly, she started drawing Dawn into the bed. A part of her wanted to say nothing more gentle than "get out," but for the sake of their future encounters, if there were to be any, and for the safety of anyone else Dawn might play with, Lori knew she had to talk.

"Let's get some sleep now," she said, "we'll talk tomorrow when you take me out for a big, expensive breakfast at the Hilton."

"Sure," Dawn answered, completely *unsure* of everything for just about the first time she could remember.

They slept, but probably not peacefully, and the next day they talked endlessly. Or, at least, Lori talked.

"Doing SM is not the same thing as defending yourself, you know. I wasn't going to fight back or hurt you in any way, so you didn't need to just clobber me or beat me down. There are a lot of people who confuse SM and abuse, one way and another. They beat their partners, as you beat me last night....."

Dawn interrupted. "But that was what you wanted. That's what we've been talking about all this time."

"To some extent, you're right. It's my fault. I could have and obviously *should* have made everything much more clear, but I suppose I was trying not to make it too clinical. Maybe I was also assuming that some natural instinct would take over and guide you by... by magic, I guess."

"Magic?" Dawn whispered the word, trying to give it a comic tone to lighten things up. "No," she added, "magic didn't happen." Dawn whispered the last part, hoping it was only to herself.

"No, it did not happen. But, think about it. What's spousal abuse? It's when one person beats another person they say they care about, but they do it without making sure that the other person gets what they want out of it. They do it without consent. That's the key: consent."

"I'm trying to see where you're going with this, but I had your consent, didn't I? Even if I did it wrong, it was what you wanted. And, besides, nobody else ever complained. So, I'm only guilty of being bad at what we did compared to other people you know, not of abusing you. Hey, you know, this is kind of making me mad, and that's not a process I want to do with you. You know I care about you, so just tell me what I did wrong. It won't go that way again... you... I promise you that."

"You're right. I've started this out all wrong. You need to understand what's SM and what's abuse, not because of us and what we did. You need to understand *that* for your own sake, and for the women you may play with in the future. Our problem... you understand we *do* have a problem... is something else. Let me try again. I'll give you a couple of 'position papers' about SM and abuse, but we need to talk about the difference between the pounding you gave me last night and the scene I expected. Please, don't get angry. Believe me, if anyone *should* be angry, it isn't you."

"So," Dawn started, keeping Lori's attention by holding one hand in the air between them. "So, you're like mad at me because I didn't know what you wanted. You're mad because I did what you said you wanted done instead of something you kept all secret and never told me at all. Is that it? Well, that's crap!" In those few words, Dawn had gone from confused to furious, and she was on the brink of getting up to leave when Lori's patented "hurt-me" smile stopped her. "OK," she said, "you got me, but talk fast, this isn't going over that big with me."

"Fine, Dawn, just let me talk, will you. I'm not blaming you. I still like you a lot. I still hope that you will want to try again, but maybe not right away. So, let's not talk about SM like that, I'll get you some stuff about it. Let's just talk about last night, about flogging."

Dawn tried to look settled and calm and interested, but it was far from easy. She was definitely not in the habit of letting women... of letting *anyone* tell her what to do and how. But this was Lori, so she'd at least try.

"OK, where to begin. Well, at the beginning, I guess: Everything was fine, I was glad to be with you and very excited about sharing the intimacy and the high of a flogging with you. I wanted to give you that, if you know what I mean. And, yes, I wanted to have that... but it's different, still... I wanted to have that from you, specifically from *you*. And everything really was fine, the mood was there, I was getting wet and feeling something great was about to happen. The cold bench against my skin is always a reminder of the best times, and that helped. The shackles on my wrists were good. I mean, really... it was perfect until...."

Lori looked at Dawn, this was where the land-mine would be buried, she knew that. Still, it had to be said. "Perfect, until you started to hit me with the first flogger." She stopped. As she expected, she was rapidly losing Dawn's attention. "Yes?" she asked, as kittenish as she was able.

"So, everything was cool while I was just doing exactly what you'd set up, then everything was bad as soon as I started to do what we were there for. You know, I think *you're* the confused one, girlie!"

"No, Dawn, no one is confused. I just didn't know you were inexp... no, I misjudged your prepar.... no, really, I have to say it right out: You don't know how to flog, but you *could* know and you'll find it's worth learning to do it right."

Dawn was no longer even pretending to be in a listening mood. She crossed her arms, plopped her elbows on the tabletop and stared, maybe even glared at Lori. She said nothing, so Lori continued. "Dawn, please, forgive me if I overstep here, but I just have to explain, and I really do know some things you don't, and they are things I really want you to know, so... may I?"

"Shoot. This feels big, and I'm ready to listen, just don't expect any reaction 'cause I'm on board *just* to listen. You OK with that?"

"OK with being listened to? Yeah, it's not usually what I look forward to, but here goes: When you want to flog me, I need to be warmed up to do it. Getting me sexually aroused is not a warm-up for flogging, as much as I appreciate that. To warm me, you need to give me some easy strokes and give me a chance to 'get used to' the action. If you watch me closely, you'll see me ease into the scene and the stimulation. I know, that doesn't answer the impulse you would be having to beat the shit out of me, but there's a way to see it as your own self-serving issue too. If you get me into it, you can go much further than you will by barging forward without preparing me.

"And, what I said about watching me to see when I'm warmed up and ready to move along to the next whip or to whatever you have in mind... that's *not* about me taking the control of the scene from you. It's about giving you the best and most intense scene I am able. I know, it doesn't sound that way, and the only way you'll know it's true is by *doing it* even if that means doing it 'my way.' By reading my reactions, you'll always know how much more I am ready to take for you, see? For you... or whether I can handle *any* more at that moment. I am not a Top, so I can't explain that, but Tops tell me that it is actually very easy, at least with me. They also tell me that this is something that you learn better and better with experience, once you know about it. I have to admit that part of what I know about reading the bottom's reaction – although it agrees with what Tops say – comes from feeling that I know when I am being correctly and attentively read and when that is not happening.

"After a decent warm-up that leads me to *want* something heavier or more or whatever, the same process happens over and over in the course of the scene. As the action goes along, you can know by seeing what you are getting from me whether it is safe and right to move on to heavier action or a harder tool. Are you understanding this?"

Dawn just nodded, reminding Lori with her physical attitude more than anything else that she had promised to *listen* and just listen.

"The other process that goes on in a flogging or any SM scene besides the warming up and step-to-step work is giving some kind of shape to the scene. It isn't just a matter of beating on me until you're tired, it's a matter – for both of us – of giving the scene a beginning, a middle, a peak and a natural end or a 'cool down' activity. The shape can be entirely your own. If you feel like it needs to move fast to a high level and hang there for a while before coming down quickly, you can do that... by reading and learning to direct my reactions as you work. In the same way, you could decide to ease slowly into the scene, to put its central focus on 'getting away' with a longer beating with a specific tool that interests you, one that gets you the response you want, before slowly coming down... and bringing me down. That's your choice too. By reading my responses, which I promise are completely honest and unedited, you can have the scene you want and give me a scene that I will be satisfied by at the same time.

"I can even understand that there might be times when your plan would be to go through the scene and stop somewhere that I wouldn't understand as 'being brought down' or being 'cooled down' from the peak. That's your choice too, so long as there is something I can hold on to, something that makes me believe that you really are in charge of the scene, and that you are doing something intentional and... tech.... Wow, this is hard. But, if you do the technical part well, you'll have my trust and that will allow me to relax, and to let you do what you are doing without doubts or second-guessing or giving up.... as I did last night.

"After you stopped – I wish I could say 'after the scene,' but you know I don't believe I can call that a scene – you did something really right... but for the wrong reason, and maybe with bad timing too. You asked if I was OK. Remember? Well, let me tell you, that's good. I like that, and every bottom I know does too, but we need a moment to know *your* feelings first and to find out our own feelings after the action has stopped. We need to have already heard that we did all right, for *you*... I mean, if we... or, if I did do all right. Well, then we're ready to put our attention on ourselves.

"Anyway, let me make this clear. At the end, if you would have told me, as you did, that the scene with me was worth waiting for, then given me a moment to process your happiness with the action... well, maybe I would have found a way to justify and clarify my own feelings *for the sake of your pleasure*, and we wouldn't be having this talk now. But, you know, that would *not* be so good. This talk is good, and I'm glad it's happening and I hope you will feel that way in the end too."

Lori felt sure it would be a mistake to stop and expect any response from Dawn at this point, but she remained silent for a moment anyway. Dawn stuck by her guns by remaining not impassive but silent. She was listening.

"You understand that what I mean is that I need at least a moment between the flogging and the question of whether I am OK. You could have me pick up the whips, or order me to leave the room to look at my marks. You could just excuse yourself for a minute or two, maybe go to the bathroom or take a moment to put on some of your clothes or whatever. It's just about staying in the scene mood a little while but leaving me on my own, untouched and unquestioned. It's a small thing, really, but it matters to me.

"After that... well, after that, it's a good idea to actually ask if I am OK, as you did. And then, I always like it if a Top also gives a call or drops by or something to be sure I'm still OK a day or two later. Tops I have played with before have usually done this second check-in by kind of calling to ask me if I'd like to see them again. It works. If I figured out that the scene didn't work for me, I'd probably just say I didn't care to repeat it, but I could be polite, you know. It's not exactly a rule about calling later, you know, but I appreciate it."

The women just sat for a few minutes. They looked at each other most of the time, but they turned away in embarrassment sometimes. Clearly, they were fine, both of them, and they were on their way to planning another shot at the flogging scene. They still had more than 24 hours before Dawn's lover would be home.

In fact, they did do another scene. Apparently Lori's "injuries" were more emotional than physical, and they were helped, even cured, by the opportunity to talk. The second scene went better, but a bit clumsily as Dawn checked in far too often to be sure she was doing what was needed. Shortly after that weekend, Lori provided Dawn with a position statement from the National Coalition for Sexual Freedom on SM and Abuse. And, just in case, she enclosed a notice of an upcoming leatherfest with a red circle around the Flogging 101 and Flogging 201 classes. Dawn thought about attending the classes without telling Lori, but just out of gratitude, she decided to be up-front about it. In fact, Lori decided – as if it were a new idea for her – to attend both classes with Dawn. After all, the 201 class description invited students to bring their own whips and bottoms, and Dawn owned no whips of her own.

SCENE THREE EXAMINED

MAKING A FLOGGING AND MAKING IT WORK

NEGOTIATING DOESN'T ALWAYS WORK. LORI and Dawn "negotiated" for a long time, and still ended up with a mess on their hands. Maybe magic works, maybe miracles happen, and maybe there are absolutely natural Tops who need no training at all. And, maybe not! In any case, most of us have to have some guidance. We also need, as Lori tried to tell Dawn, to have an idea of what a scene is.

A flogging is a whole thing in and of itself, it is not just x many of this stroke followed by this many minutes of that stroke using flogger A to stimulate body part C. It might be that the way to understand a flogging scene in a holistic way is to think of it as a story being either told by the Top or made up together by the Top and the bottom. Already, you have two different – both very workable – concepts of how a scene is built just there.

A story has a beginning in which the characters explain themselves, their relationships and their intentions. It has a middle where they work at their intended goal up to some kind of peak of activity or emotion. Then, it has a denouement, a controlled ending, in which the pace slows to a stop and everyone absorbs the lessons or changes or facts the story is about. The way this translates into scene-building is obvious.

Another view of scene-building that works for some people is to see the scene as a musical composition, as described in the introductory chapter of this book.

Whether it is compared to a story or a musical composition, and whether it is planned or runs on the experienced habits of the players, a good scene requires some kind of intention (fantasy, sexual connection, pleasure, test limits, try out a new instrument, whatever), some preparation (at least getting the people and materials together in a workable way), then a warm-up, action that rises to a peak, and an ending (however gentle or abrupt).

You won't go far wrong in understanding the technique of building any SM scene if you allow yourself to use an analogy as easily applicable as the ones above, but the "art" in flogging comes from the fact that, once you have the science (a.k.a. technique) down, you can invent and improvise and be creative and spontaneous.

And, no amount of planning or perfectly honed technique will guarantee that every scene will go nicely and please everyone. Sometimes, things don't work so well.

THINKING OF THINGS THAT CAN GO WRONG

If you accept that sooner or later something will go wrong, then you will be ready to have scenes that go right. If you have your first-aid kit on hand, for instance, you are all the more ready to have scenes that never need it.

Unwanted pain is an issue, maybe even a funny one sometimes, but it can be very serious at times. There is nothing more uncomfortable for a bottom than stubbing her toe while being flogged. Try as we will, once in a while there will be some instance of toe-stubbing pain from some source or other during a scene. It is a question of knowing that it can happen, knowing you've done what you can to prevent it, and freely admitting that it has happened when it does... then going on as quickly as possible with the scene. There is no need in most cases for the dominant and submissive roles or attitudes to be abandoned when an unintended pain happens nor for a great deal of discussion to take place – that can come later if needed – but, as soon as the pain source has been removed, the scene should pick up as near as possible to where it left off.

If a restraint has become painful and must be adjusted, the cross twisted back a bit from the wall or whatever, it can all be done, in most cases, without really letting the scene come to a full stop. In some dynamics, the preposterous "blaming" of the bottom keeps things going. For other couples or at other times, this would be a deal-breaker and scene-ender. You have to trust your instincts.

Oops! is not, contrary to popular (if humorous) wisdom, the Top's safe word, but Tops do make mistakes. If the flogger wraps around and stings skin that was not intended to be flogged, for example, it is seldom a good idea for the Top to see it happen and just ignore it. Neither is "oops" often an adequate response. Nonetheless, if the Top acknowledges the mistake in a way that the bottom understands instantly, there is usually no real break in the scene. Frequently, just reaching out to touch the unintended welt *gently* is enough. A Top who figures, "Oh, well, she wanted to be hit," and ignores the error, is building up a barrier of doubt where a clear field of trust is required. They are, in a small way, becoming Dawn-like.

Checking in with a bottom, especially if it is done often or too late in the scene, can ruin the experience for both players. Instead of asking the bottom if all is well, a Top should learn to read the bottom's skin responses and muscular reactions, and to correctly interpret the bottom's vocalizations and words. Checking in as a scene gets started, particularly where previously untried or unreliable restraints are in use (or some other dubious factor is present) may be useful. Once the scene is up and running, however, it ought to be possible for the feedback loop to become verbal only in case of an emergency. Granted, some bottoms like being begged for approval and some Tops love being told they're doing a good job with their floggers. With any luck at all, such people will find each other and leave everyone else alone.

Public-utility attitude is a deadly disease that infects some Tops and is, sadly, appreciated by some bottoms. What is that? It is the idea that a Top is or ought to be a public utility, a service provided for bottoms such that they can turn him on like an electric fan or a water faucet and get the expected "utility" (flogging) until they've had enough and are ready to turn it off. Infected Tops are often called "service tops." The bottom's converse of this syndrome is called being "pushy" or a "do-me" bottom. Either way, the fact is that flogging can be a full-scale communication, a full-on erotic encounter, and at best, a shared ecstatic experience, but these things are impossible with service Tops and pushy bottoms or any other variant of the public-utility attitude.

As with everything else that most players might consider "wrong," of course, there are couples for whom these attitudes work beautifully. If the bottom is the dominant personality in a pair, it may even be the only way flogging will ever take place. Still, public-utility attitude has to be displayed up front and acknowledged (very likely not in that language) if people who don't already know each other extremely well are going to be able to play in this atmosphere.

Isolated arrogance is the opposite of public-utility thinking, but it is also a disease. A Top who feels superior to all bottoms or even just to the bottom he is doing a flogging with at this moment isolates himself on a pedestal at which only *he* worships. That's OK for him because he wouldn't value anyone else's opinion or praise all that much anyway. What do the opinions of mere mortals mean to a self-recognized god, especially if the mortals in question are bottoms? Obviously, the same attitude can be present in a bottom who then feels that she is casting pearls before swine every time she deigns to submit to a scene with any Top.

Even if everyone around you suffers from one of these mental disorders, resist them – because a good flogging is simply not a realistic possibility when a public utility, pushy bottom, self-recognized god or too-good-for-*your*-touch bottom is in the scene.

Mismatched couples: Regardless of mutual attraction and even the lustiest shared desires, couples can be mismatched in any number of ways. The obvious ways are quickly recognized and usually circumvented: They're both Tops or both bottoms; he only does fire and piercing, she only wants flogging and caning, etc. But some mismatches just are not that easily detected or avoided.

Sometimes the problem that prevents two people from fitting together, especially in a scene like flogging with such potential for real intimacy, is simply what is called "chemistry." You hear it sometimes, "I don't know what it is, I like him just fine, but I don't want to play with him." Well, sometimes this mismatch of persons is not obvious until there is a scene in progress. You will have to decide for yourself, but unless you're getting something really wonderful out of the scene (relief after months of not being flogged or having no one to flog), it would seem that the best thing to do is call a stop to the scene as soon as you know it can't go *really* right. And, if you discover during or after a flogging scene that you and your partner were a bad match, blame the bad match... don't blame the partner or the flogging or yourself.

There are other reasons why two people might not be a good match, of course. People whose SM is done in different "flavors" might find the difference insurmountable. For example, someone who thinks of flogging as love-making would surely have trouble settling into a scene with someone whose approach is "I have a right to punish and use you as I will." Both of these "flavors" and several dozen others are encountered among experienced players, and compromises or accommodations are sometimes possible. Often, however, the gap can not be bridged, and it is unlikely that a good flogging will result from an interaction where either party just "changes flavors" to please the other.

Bad circumstances, like the wrong equipment being all that is available or poor timing or the wrong background music, and any other unfortunate happenstance can ruin a flogging. The best thing to do, if you're not sure the circumstances are in order all around, is postpone the scene. Trying to make the best of imperfect circumstances leads to making do with an imperfect flogging. That's seldom a worthwhile effort.

Actual emergencies can happen. Bottoms are rarely injured in any way that creates an emergency during a flogging scene. It's not impossible, just not likely. Still, heart attacks and earthquakes and fires and sudden breakdowns of equipment can happen. Bondage can go wrong. Managing emergencies that happen during a flogging is not different than managing the same circumstances at any other time. The only special arrangements that are advisable are simple ones:

- *Seriously consider taking CPR and First Aid Classes now!*
- Have current and adequate first aid supplies or kit, at hand.
- Have the medications each player might need because of existing conditions at hand.

- Never do a flogging with the bottom in *truly* inescapable bondage. (What if the Top has a heart attack?) OK, "never" may be a bit strong, but it is not that difficult to do bondage that can be escaped after some degree of effort or time, and there are ways to have totally inescapable bondage made "escapable," too. One simple method is the "safe call" system.

  A "safe call" is set up, usually by the bottom. It means having someone who is not going to be present during the scene know where the scene is taking place, and promising that they will receive a phone call at a certain time telling them the bottom is safe, presumably after the scene. By having a safe call in place, the bottom who can not free herself can know that a friend will come looking for her after a certain time. However uncomfortable it may be to remain in bondage until the appointed hour, this gives inescapable bondage a safety factor that covers even the most extreme situations – like the sudden incapacity of the Top.

- Take good care of your floggers and other whips so they will work as intended.

- No matter where you are, know how to get a 911 or other emergency call through.

- *And, no matter what happens, stay as calm as possible to be as effective as possible!*

Psychological barriers are sometimes encountered. Even if this problem is talked about a great deal more often than the facts of life would support, it can be quite real. People worry endlessly about running into some submerged memory of child abuse during a scene – and flogging, because it looks like some relatively common abuse methods, is more suspect than most other SM in this connection. On the other hand, only a handful of people can tell firsthand stories of anything of the sort actually taking place. In any case, when someone reports having a psychological problem because of abuse or memory issues, the flogging partner (Top or bottom) should remember that he is *not* that person's psychiatrist. If you are that partner, do not attempt to fix the problem. Instead, demand that the psychologically confronted person get professional help before you get together to do another flogging. Meantime, even the emergency care for this kind of problem is probably not something you can not do on the spot. Let it go, let the scene stop, help the person get home or to a hospital or wherever they say they feel they need to be.

Under the direction of a professional counselor or psychiatrist, you may later be asked to join a discussion or to give the distressed person a chance to talk to you. Try to accommodate this request, but only if you are able to do so comfortably and without significant personal risk of any kind.

Lack of technical expertise is a big issue in SM. This, of course, was Dawn's problem. Many people believe that they are good Tops or good bottoms and that, for reasons beyond explanation, they need no training to be very good in whatever scene they choose to do. The good news for us, since our interest is in flogging, is that most of these people really can learn from experience and from us. Even so, the inexperienced and untrained Tops may leave a trail of unhappy bottoms in their wake and the unready bottoms will disappoint Tops for a while too.

As Lori told Dawn, there are classes all over the country all the time, maybe not this weekend and maybe not in your county, but soon and not so very far away. Finding the classes may present some difficulty for a person with few or no connections to the organized leather/SM community. But with a connection to the Internet, it becomes much easier. Searching under BDSM, for instance, will mostly result in porn sites, but adding "events" to the search criteria will usually

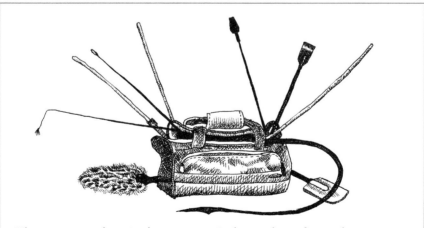

When it comes to toybags, size does not matter. Far better to have a few toys that you can use excellently than a huge collection with which you are less than competent.

turn up some gatherings at which there will be instructional sessions and demon-
strations. Even with the World Wide Web and practice search techniques, you
may have some trouble finding classes, but getting connected in the real world is
usually possible by visiting any major city and going to the local fetish leather
store. There are likely to be notices and flyers in the shop, and the local under-
ground or gay and lesbian newspapers are almost sure to be available as well. It
doesn't matter that you may be completely heterosexual, look at the gay papers.
Often, the gay press is only place sexual matters, including SM events, are adver-
tised.

Clubs may be mentioned on flyers or in ads, and it is often productive to
get in touch with a club even through a voice-mail-only system. Club members
may be found in leather bars, often recognizable as club members because they
are wearing back patches with (often quite explicit) insignia on them. Granted,
again, the ads and the clubs and the leather bars are often gay, but they are almost
as often very accepting of the fact that you are not. In any case, many gay club
members will know about pansexual (for all orientations) or heterosexual connections in their community (or yours) as well.

If all else fails, there are many large gatherings of leatherfolk each year that
are easily found on the Internet or through personal contacts, and attending one
of these larger events will give you ample opportunity to discover what is happening in your own area and who you need to know to be kept informed. The
biggest (and among the best) events most years include: The National Leather
Association's Living in Leather conference, currently scheduled for July and moving from city to city; the anniversary of Black Rose in Washington, DC, each fall;
Leather University's Dungeon 101, 201, etc. (up to 601 in 2001) that take place
in Fort Lauderdale each October; and Thunder in the Mountains in Denver
every summer. Classes and opportunities to play in supervised surroundings are
provided by all these events, and the ones mentioned here are all safe places for
people of all sexes, orientations and levels of experience.

CONSIDERING AFTERCARE

What is required or useful in the way of after-care for flogging bottoms is
different depending on the circumstances of the flogging, the intensity of the

scene and the relationship between the two players. After-care includes physical treatment of the flogged area and psychological/emotional attention to the bottom. It may also include "community care" in some cases.

Physical aftercare is relatively simple in almost all cases. In fact, less is better. If possible, washing the flogged area under running water is a good idea, mostly to flush away any foreign materials that may have become embedded in the marks and cuts or on the sticky skin. It is not a good idea to apply antibiotic ointment (unless you are hoping to increase scarring) or to bandage the area (which would usually be very clumsy, anyway). Air-drying is recommended. For comfort, air-drying with a T-shirt or other light garment over the area is also very acceptable. If the flogged area is dirty, as it could be if the scene happened outdoors in the wind or the whips were kept at hand by leaving them on the floor, showering or flushing the area is especially important.

The idea that antibiotic ointments, some of which advertise that they reduce the appearance of scars, would actually *increase* scarring may be a bit of a surprise. The reason is simple: Most of the bleeding associated with flogging is from very superficial wounds and from swollen (leathered up) skin. When the swelling goes down, the wound will usually close completely, allowing the original skin to knit immediately without scarring. Any ointment or bandage will prevents the natural and immediate reconnecting of the disrupted skin surface, and will increase the likelihood of scarring. If a wound is not entirely superficial, there is likely to be a scar anyway, so you may choose to use an ointment or other medication. The ads that promise less scarring are always specific about this being true when the ointment is used on "scrapes," meaning wounds where skin has been removed and the edges are no longer able to close up without generating new skin cells.

If there is bleeding, it will probably stop on its own soon after the flogging stops. If it doesn't or if the bleeding is profuse (which is very rare), apply pressure to the bleeding wound site for a minute or so using a clean, dry cloth. The pressure will help slow the blood flow and give the blood at the site a better chance to clot successfully. Refer to a first aid manual or medical professional if dry pressure is not sufficient to stop a wound from bleeding.

Two doctors, two manuals and one paramedic were all presented with the question of how long the dry cloth pressure should be applied to stop bleeding (in effect, how long bleeding should be tolerated without concern). Their answers varied remarkably from one minute to 15 minutes, but they all agreed that if the cloth you are pressing with become blood-soaked, you should add more cloth on top of it rather than remove or replace it – the idea being that by removing the cloth you would also be removing the clotted blood and starting the process over each time.

Bruises are an interesting question for flogging fans. Some want to keep the marks as long as possible and have as much marking as possible, others want as little marking as they can arrange and want to have the marks fade as soon as possible. Rather than reinvent a wheel that was not all that easily carved the first time, here is the result of my research as published in *Leathersex Q & A* (Daedalus Publishing Company, 1996):

A friend of mine, Ben, recently told me how he takes control of the bruises by choosing to bathe in hot water (to increase bruising) or cold (to reduce bruising) immediately after a scene. I have no idea how effective Ben's method is, but it pleases him. Of course, his intention is usually to increase and retain bruises, so I doubt he has tried very hard to reduce or prevent them.

While leathersex players are always my first reference points for information about leathersex, I sometimes refer to outside sources as well. In this case, I looked at *The Doctor's Book of Home Remedies*, compiled and published by *Prevention Magazine*, 1990. The advice there is a fire-and-ice treatment like Ben's. The editors, referring to information provided by some pretty high-octane doctors, suggest that chilling a potential bruise site with ice helps reduce or prevent bruising. They say you need to start chilling the bruise site right away, and continue for 24 hours, chilling it for 15 minutes at a time, then letting it warm itself up naturally before reapplying the ice. After 24 hours of chilling to constrict the blood vessels and reduce the scope of the bruising, they tell us to switch from ice to heat. The heat, of course, dilates the blood vessels, improving circulation and healing. They also suggest that if it is possible, you can reduce bruising by elevating the bruised area, using gravity to help drain the internally spilled blood from the bruise site.

If you want to reduce your tendency to bruise in a continuous way, the doctors quoted in Home Remedies recommend that you take vitamin C. They say you should check with your own doctor before taking major doses of the vitamin, of course, but their suggestion is a usually-safe dosage of 500 milligrams three times a day.

A friend of mine who ought to know adds that bleeding/bruising is also increased by taking regular aspirin or vitamin E within 24 hours before or 48 hours after the event. So, avoiding aspirin and vitamin E, or choosing to take them, may give you some control of the bruising and marking.

Finally, the Home Remedy doctors point out that alcoholics, drug abusers, people taking many kinds of prescription medications, or even aspirin are going to bruise more easily and/or more severely than others. This is based on simple medical facts such as that medications often include desirable anti-clotting or blood-thinning effects or side-effects, and blood that flows more readily or more freely means bruises that develop more rapidly and clear up more slowly.

Aftercare for the mind, heart, spirit is also simple, even if some people find it bothersome. At the end of the flogging, it should somehow be possible to be in physical contact. Both partners are likely to appreciate this. The bottom often needs a degree of assurance that he has performed well, that the beating was intended to please him and that it also pleased the Top. The Top similarly needs to know that the bottom is OK, does not feel resentment or anger for what has just taken place and is pleased with the scene as she performed it. This can usually be accomplished with simple, tender contact... no words required.

Many bottoms feel as Lori told Dawn that she feels: A few moments of quiet are needed between the last stroke and the inquiry as to how the bottom feels. In an earlier chapter, Dennis and mark met this need by allowing mark to cling to Dennis' boots until he was ready to move back into the "real world." In the first chapter, Jim held and kissed Leila and let her cry a bit, then opened the post-scene dialogue by actually asking her what kind of aftercare she wanted.

Commonly, after a few minutes, the Top might ask the bottom to verbalize an answer to the simple question, "Are you all right?" The answer will almost always be in the affirmative, and the question should be cast to make this answer as easy as possible. Don't ask, for instance, "Is anything wrong, now?"

If conditions permit and she is welcome to do so, the Top should stay with the bottom for a while, through the clean-up and such. If this is not possible or practical, the Top should definitely verbalize a recognition of the fact that it is not possible. Or, if the interpersonal dynamics include the bottom "serving" the Top, the Top may wish to signal recognition that the clean-up represents a form of service, just to ensure that the desired dynamic is in effect.

When the scene has been light relative to the capabilities of the bottom, this may be all the after-care that is needed.

When the scene has been other than very light or the Top and bottom are relative strangers, it is a good idea to try to arrange to at least speak by phone a day or two later. This should be the responsibility of the Top, but if the bottom (for reasons of privacy or whatever) wishes not to be available to be called or seen by the Top, then the Top should provide the bottom with a way to reach him or her. If, for example, the Top gives the bottom a phone number, then doesn't hear from him, she is relatively safe in assuming that all is well.

What do you do or say in this later check-in? Nothing in particular. The purpose is to give the bottom an opportunity to voice any questions or concerns that may have come up. The real test, if it is reasonable, is for the Top to offer to repeat the scene at a future time. If the bottom says that's a good idea, everything must be all right. If the bottom doesn't want that to happen, keep the conversation open for at least a few minutes to give him a chance to formulate a reason for his reticence. If nothing else is said, a very courteous Top will be sure the bottom knows that it would be OK to check back with the Top again if it would be useful.

Again, neither Tops nor bottoms are meant to play psychologist or psychiatrist. That is not the purpose of after-care and it is not what flogging is for. The idea here is to take responsibility and show that you care. If an explanation is needed, you'll give it. If there was some particular moment in the scene when one partner felt something may have gone badly, it may need discussing. Most often, there is nothing to say but "Thank you." On the other hand, that is probably reason enough to be in touch.

SCENE FOUR

MISTRESS K
AND SLAVE 2

MISTRESS K WAS GIVEN SLAVE 2 – HER second slave – as a gift from another goddess who understood that she needed more service and even more worship than any one slave could possibly provide. The other reason for the gift and the other purpose of 2 was that he had already been trained to serve as the third party in certain types of Pro-Domme scenes that Selena, K's friend, no longer did – scenes that were becoming a staple in K's business. In any case, 2 had no hurt feelings about being given away. He is slave, he never even used an article such as "a" slave or *certainly* not "the" slave to describe himself. He is slave as air is air and meat is meat. He is not specific as *a* particular vase or a dog or a person is.

This evening, 2 is cleaning Mistress K's whips. They are seldom bloodied in her professional scenes. In fact, there they are more for threatening than beating. In his private service to Mistress K, 2 often bleeds on the whips. He always cleans them all, only very privately noticing the difference between those with which he has been punished and those he has seen used only in her studio. All the whips, as valued possessions of his Mistress, deserve his complete attention. All of them should be as supple and clean as possible, their lives extended by his care, their appearance improved by his ministrations.

Naked, as he always is except when running errands outside, he kneels on the floor of the studio, the whips ranged and grouped on one side of his knees, his supplies on the other. His instructions had been very specific as things tended to be with Mistress K. "Prepare to clean the whips, 2," she had said.

He was fully prepared. He had been fully prepared for nearly 30 minutes, but he remained kneeling and waiting for further instructions.

At last, Mistress K entered the room. She was wearing very high, navy blue heels and dark blue stockings with heavy seams teased into perfectly straight lines up the backs of her legs. That was all 2 could see with his head bowed, as it always was when he was in his waiting position. He waited in the hope of seeing those adored feet stop in front of him. If Mistress should stop in the space before him and facing him, he would be permitted to fall forward and kiss her shoes, keeping his hands linked behind his back. The deep, forward bend would be painful to raise out of, but Mistress K never stayed around to see how he struggled with that. If she stopped and turned to face away, he was trained to slide forward onto all fours, ready to crawl behind her wherever she may lead him. He hoped he would be permitted to kiss her feet and get on with his work, but he would accept with complete equanimity being moved along to a punishment or another task, or just crawling around behind Mistress for a while until she led him back to the cleaning of the whips.

After walking around the arrangement of slave, whips and cleaning supplies a couple of times, Mistress K stopped in front of 2, facing him. Without the slightest hesitation, he dropped his face to the floor between the toes of her dark, pointed shoes. "Kiss," she ordered. With slow deliberation, 2 raised his head about two inches from the floor, froze tightly, then turned his head first right, then left, leaving the slightest and most loving kiss possible on each shoe. "Continue," Mistress K snapped as she pulled her feet away from 2's face and turned to leave.

It took him a moment. The joy of Her attention in this way always left him a little dazed and, besides, his back no longer responded instantly to the internal command to lift his body upright. In a moment, he cleared his head and, teetering from side to side a bit, straightened into a kneeling position again. As he settled, he stretched his back and looked over the items arranged on the floor around himself.

There was a lot of work here: a horsehair whip, three regular flat-tailed floggers, a flat-braided flogger, a rubber paddle, a hardwood paddle, a braided cat-o-nine tails, two single-tailed whips, a sjambok, a rattan cane, and a suede "duster" as Mistress called it. The "duster" was always a challenge. He expected no blood on anything except the crackers of the single-tail whips, but he was prepared for anything.

On the other side of his bent legs he had a small plastic trough of water he hoped was still warm, bottles of peroxide, dishwashing liquid, Simple Green and Murphy's Oil Soap; a tube of leather dressing, a tiny bottle of stain remover for suede, a strong plastic hairbrush, an empty shot glass and a small, pillow-like cloth square filled with a suede-cleaning powder, several towels, a few smaller rags and a small, natural sponge. A normal cellulose or artificial sponge would no doubt have done the job just as well, but he felt that spending the extra time to find a natural sponge and the extra money to buy it showed his respect for the tools of Mistress's trade and the instruments of Her pleasure.

2 didn't expect to use all the equipment and supplies, he never used everything, but he was always prepared for anything. This day he did not need the Simple Green – a grease-cutting liquid cleanser he used for stubborn stains – or the shot glass, which was sometimes used to dip single-tail crackers or the tips of leather floggers if they needed real washing.

Spreading a large towel in front of himself, 2 began. He decided to have the paddles done first. They were easy and, in a sense, plain work. With the whips he took a more sensual pleasure. Just handling them was somehow an honor. The paddles, on the other hand, were simply rubber and wood to be kept clean. He put both paddles on the towel. He wet the sponge in peroxide and drizzled the surfaces of the paddles with peroxide watching for the fizz that would mean blood to be cleaned away. There was none, so he quickly wiped the paddles down with the towel. Then he slipped the rubber paddle into the trough of water.

Yes, the water was still warm, but he knew that it would work as well if it cooled, it would just be less pleasant to work with.

He dipped a rag into the water, squeezed it nearly dry and poured a small amount of the oil soap on it. He worked the soap into the rag and rubbed hard as he cleaned the wooden paddle end to end with the soapy rag. He repeatedly dipped the rag into the water, squeezed it nearly dry, and wiped the paddle again. When, after three or four repetitions, there was no soap at all left in the rag, he wiped the paddle more gently with the damp cloth, trying to leave no line or mark on the shiny wood, then he buffed the paddle dry using another clean towel.

Carefully arching his body over the cleaning supplies, 2 was able to stretch out and place the paddle on the inspection bench near the wall. Just as he put the paddle down, She spoke: "Too tired to get up and move, are you, 2?" He knew. He didn't have to hear her to know that this indecorous twisting and stretching of his body was not the way to do the job.

"Sorry, Ma'am," he said, pulling the paddle back with the same hand that had, a split second earlier, put it down. He knelt with the paddle across his thighs and his head bowed.

"You never know when you are watched, 2. And, I know you anyway. I know you will take a shortcut when you can. Watched or not, slave, you are not to take the easy way, it is not your place. You should be always seeking to provide me with ease and to perform in the most precise way you are able. There is no sense in which pushing a paddle onto a bench from four feet away is the most precise way of placing it there. You understand?"

"Yes, Ma'am."

"Has this manhandling left hand prints or marks on the paddle? If so, clean them away *now!*"

There was, in fact, a hand print in the middle of the paddle from where 2 gripped it tightly as he drew it back. He picked up the buffing towel and wiped the paddle to a shine, leaving its handle enveloped in the edge of the towel and gripped lightly in his left hand, its other end resting even more lightly on his towel-covered right hand. He waited. She said nothing, but he was not to follow orders he assumed he would be given. He had learned that lesson. So, he waited.

At last, She spoke: "Now, let me see with what respect you can properly place that paddle on the bench to present it to your Mistress."

The paddle might as well have been the fabled Chalice of Christ for all the intense attention 2 gave it as he rose slowly, in one painfully controlled motion. He backed out of the niche between whips and cleaning supplies, and turned carefully, making sure not to turn his back on the place where he believed Mistress K to be on the other side of the room. He took two short steps, bent, and slid the paddle across his right hand, onto the bench, not letting it scrape or make the slightest sound.

"I see," Mistress K said, "my tools are not worth the effort to stand and take two steps if I am not here to remind you. Well, 2, be reminded that everything of mine is perfect, everything I own except you. And you *will* continue to work on yourself and strive to be as perfect for me as that paddle is. Look at it!" Still bent over the bench, the paddle no more than a two feet from his face, 2 bent closer and examined the mirror perfect finish of the dark wood. "I am giving you the kind of use and training that will one day make you as excellent as that lovely, African wood... I am trying, anyway. You will try as hard as I do. You know what is right, 2. Do that! Every time, even if you imagine I am not watching."

"Yes, Ma'am," 2 whispered. Suddenly he regretted the whisper. He should have spoken up. This time, though, Mistress accepted his contrition for what it was. He heard her heels snapping against the floor as she left the room. He also heard that she did not close the studio door.

He returned to his place and knelt, his attention now Zen-like in its focus. As he stepped, he thought only of stepping. As he bent, he had no thought but bending. As his knees met the floor, he experienced only the reliable support of the floor. Then, not overly slowed by the heightened state, but extremely careful to maintain it, he went back to work.

2 lifted the rubber paddle out of the water and turned it on edge in his hand. The water ran off it quickly. Even though a tiny amount of oil soap was now in the water, and oil soap is not the perfect cleanser for Mistress's rubber instruments, it would not be a problem. He dampened the washing cloth again, putting a drop or two of dishwashing liquid on it this time, a bit extra to be sure he removed all the oil soap, in fact. Then, just as he had done with the hardwood paddle, he rubbed the paddle down, dipped and squeeze-dried the cloth, wiped the paddle again, and repeated until he was sure he was working with no soap. He dried the rubber paddle with loving care then, centering himself especially

carefully as he prepared to enter the activity that had gone so wrong before, he stood, cradling the paddle on the drying towel.

A moment later he was kneeling again, pleased that he had done flawlessly what he tried before to omit altogether. For a moment, he believed himself worthy of Mistress's attention, then he realized that this – more even than the idle thoughts he might otherwise have entertained – was not the kind of attention to his work that She demanded. If 2 let himself think of himself, he was not thinking of Mistress and serving her. He was not focusing on the task she had given him. He took a breath, thinking only of that breath and its power to clear his mind of himself and return him to his work.

2 worked with great care after that. He found that his mind wandered, but all he needed to bring himself back was the reminder that became almost a prayer this time as it often did: "Do the bidding of Mistress, think of nothing else."

The "duster" would be next. He had no orders about which whips to clean before or after which, so he chose the task he liked least in order to force a greater concentration of his attention. Suede is damaged by most rough cleaning, so the duster was never used in such a way that it was likely to become soiled. It had never been bloodied. All the same, 2 held the handle of the "duster" between his clamped thighs to allow himself to examine ever inch of every tail of the flogger with great care. At a glance, anyone else would have thought the whip perfectly clean, perhaps even new. 2 saw the difference between the free, slightly fluffy nap of the untouched areas of suede and the compressed, disarranged nap of the parts of the tails that had landed on someone's skin. He found no stain, but had the stain remover available. Since he would not have to wait for the stain remover to dry, the suede flogger would go quickly.

2 caught the thought of getting the duster done quickly and knew immediately that quickly was not necessarily "perfectly." He chastised himself for the thought and for taking pleasure in the idea that he would be done sooner, then set to work with the suede-cleaning pillow. Each side of each tail was carefully brushed with the pillow from its base at the handle to its tip 20 inches out. The knot at the top of the handle was also suede. 2 gently followed each strip of suede in the knot with the corner of the pillow until he was sure he had been over the entire knot twice. To his surprise, the cleaning pillow was becoming soiled. There had been some dirt hidden in the nap of the suede.

The handle of the "duster" was shiny, chrome-tanned leather and, again, 2 saw no dirt or imperfection to clean. Nonetheless, he put a drop or two of leather dressing on his hand and worked it into the wrist strap, the hand-end knot and the shaft of the handle. Where leather met suede, he used his fingertips, even his short fingernails, to work the dressing into the leather without getting even the tiniest drop on the suede. Any leather dressing would surely stain the suede. In the eyes of Mistress, that would destroy the duster completely. After the tiny amount of dressing had been massaged into the leather and seemed to have disappeared completely, 2 buffed the leather with a clean cloth, surprising himself by picking up some of the damp dressing on the cloth. When he was first learning to take care of Mistress's whips, he always over-applied the dressing and left cloth after cloth soaked with it when he buffed the leather dry. Now, he was able to judge the amount required, or to add a drop at a time, so the cloths were really buffing more than they were soaking up excess dressing.

When, at last, all the whips were clean and set out for presentation, 2 wrapped all the cloths and towels he had used in one dry towel; he closed all the containers. After dumping the slightly sudsy water in the bathtub and using the bundled towels to wipe the tub, he put the towels in the laundry hamper and returned with the wiped-dry plastic trough. 2 put all his cleaning supplies in the trough and returned it to its place in the cupboard, then returned to his place in the middle of the now-empty floor.

Mistress K found him there, kneeling, hands linked behind his back, head down. She stood in front of him, far enough away that he could not think he was to be rewarded just then by being permitted to kiss her feet. First, she would discover what state he was in. She was in no mood for either an empty gesture or some kind of self-congratulatory move from her slave. She looked over the cleaned items displayed on the bench. The presentation was beautiful, everything at the same angle, determined by the angle at which the longest paddle had to be turned to fit entirely on the bench. The gathered tails of each flogger were draped together carefully, spaced from one another evenly, the flogger handles, matching the angle of the paddle exactly. The handle ends of the single-tail whips were at the same angle and spacing, the bellies of the whips looping off the front of the bench, the falls and crackers lined up on the bench perfectly. She was pleased. 2 would be rewarded, perhaps he would even be permitted to have some sexual pleasure this evening.

She didn't have to say the word "come," to know he would follow when she stepped close to 2, turned away from him and started walking.

2 thought of nothing but his unspoken orders. Rising to all fours, he crawled. He didn't even register the anticipated pleasure of reward or concern himself that She might have seen something worthy of punishment. He had done his work, now he would serve by being near, at her feet, following the silent command to be exactly there for Her.

Scene Four Examined

Cleaning and Maintaining Flogging Instruments

From the beginning, it is important to understand that opinions are all over the place on the subject of cleaning and maintaining leather of any sort, and all the more so where working leathers like whips are concerned. The methods mentioned in this chapter and the following examination of the chapter are known to work. Some floggers maintained as described here have been in heavy use for more than 15 years and are still in fine, if less than perfect condition. You are encouraged to continue using the products and methods that you have learned over the years if they are working well, and equally encouraged to share your ideas with the author for future reference. Opinions, even those based in experience, vary – particularly when it comes to the question of what is sufficient cleaning for a whip that may have been contaminated with HIV+ blood.

GENERAL RULES

There are few hard and fast rules about the maintenance or cleaning of leather, but some facts are generally accepted. Others can be stated with a high degree of certainty that they will not be successfully challenged. Still, most rules are, even here, statements of opinion. Here the term "working leathers" includes all instruments made of heavier than garment weights of leather and can be safely understood to include even lighter garment leather when it has been used to make a flogger. So, the basic rules:

1) Do not use garment-leather cleaners and conditioners on working leathers. The products made for clothing are often about the sheen or appearance of the leather. What is called for primarily when maintaining floggers and other working leathers is actually restoration of the moisture content of the leather. Moisture is forced out of the leather by impact action, just as water goes flying when you hit something with a wet towel. Also, garment leather, when it is cleaned, needs only the most superficial cleaning. Whips can require a cleaning that goes much deeper.

2) Do not use liquid conditioners on working leathers. Since the cowboy days of the American Wild West and before, a general rule has been not to use a conditioner on working leather which is liquid at room temperature. At a glance, this may seem a meaningless rule, but it is a valid one. Your conditioner may seem to disappear into the leather, and it really must do this to provide protection by filling spaces in which foreign material could lodge and to provide a supple condition by "oiling" the contacts between fibers. The leather and the conditioner remain together, but they are always two things sharing space. If the conditioner is liquid at room temperature, it will be driven out of the leather – and so be unable to protect the leather in any way – by impact, gravity and other common conditions.

3) Do not use leather cleaners and conditioners on non-leather materials. The products made for cleaning and conditioning leather are very specific in their formulation. It may be that they can be used on other porous materials, but (except for wood, discussed below) no other similarly porous materials are commonly used to make floggers and other SM instruments. Leather cleaners, which are formulated *not* to strip leather of its oils, will also not remove greasy residue from non-porous materials. And the oil-rich conditioners made for leather will leave a superficial coating of oil on any non-porous material they are spread over.

4) Do not permit the crackers of single-tail whips to become soaked with leather cleaners or conditioners. Crackers are commonly made of nylon or rayon threads, sometimes even cotton or cotton blends. They should be cleaned as you would clean anything else made of these materials. Warm water and mild soap are fine. They require no conditioning, and will only be made heavier and slower if they become clogged with the oils and waxes of conditioners. Besides, the conditioning materials will be thrown out of the cracker, for the most part, as soon as it is used. This means that you will be driving the oils and waxes from your conditioner into the marks made by the whip's cracker. This is not a good idea.

5) If it is necessary to use bleach on leather, use only a 10% solution and work very fast. The use of bleach on leather is a question which would never have been asked before the AIDS epidemic. Of course, we would not *want to* use bleach in any dilution at any time on leather. Now, some people are of the opinion that bleach is essential to kill HIV and other possible bio-contaminants on whips. There is a slim or nearly nil chance of there being some validity to this point of view. As far as HIV is concerned, bleach is apparently no better than air-drying as a killer of the virus. There are other bio-contaminants that are hardier, of course, such as the "bugs" that cause hepatitis. The big question is whether it is possible to collect on a whip a sufficient contaminant load to cause infection with any pathogen. Doctors tend to err on the side of caution when asked this question, but under pressure they admit that it is in the range of the often-ridiculed question of whether a mosquito could transmit HIV. That is, theoretically possible, but so unlikely as to be a meaningless question.

An even bigger question is how you would then transfer this living contaminant (in measurable quantities) to anyone else, since the contact fluids on the second person would be exiting and carrying away everything in their path.

You will decide for yourself. If you decide your own comfort or sense of safety requires the use of bleach, here's the technique: First, prepare a 10% bleach, 90% warm water solution in a glass, china or earthenware dish. Then quickly dip the affected parts of the tails of floggers and cats (and other instruments) into the solution, leaving them in just long enough to get the leather wet, but not to soak it. This will require no more than a couple of seconds. Lift the instrument away from the bleach solution and place it so that the wet portions of the tails can hang free. With a toothbrush, quickly brush the affected areas on both sides of the leather. Dip the affected leather in warm water and wiggle it about a little. Hang the tails again. Within a minute, squeeze the water out of the leather using an absorbent cloth or towel. Squeeze the leather into its original shape rather than crushing it into a wrinkled state. Allow the leather to dry completely. If it stiffens, as it almost surely will, do not be tempted to soften it by bending, wiggling and manipulating it. This will break fibers and weaken the leather. Instead, condition the leather at least once, probably twice over the next 24 hours, to make it supple again. If you have lost color, live with the change in appearance and do not attempt to re-dye the leather after each bleaching procedure. Dye tends to tighten and stiffen leather. But, if the leather is black, you may be able to regain a degree of the blackness by using black dubbin (normal clear dubbin with black pigment suspended in it) as your conditioner.

6) *Whenever it is necessary to use water on leathers, work fast, squeeze-dry immediately and allow the leather to air-dry thoroughly, then recondition.* Water, not bleach solution, should be used to remove any water-based stains that do not come off with leather cleaners and conditioners. Definitely try to remove the stains with proper leather care products before resorting to water. If water is required, work quickly and follow the instructions given above for working with bleach solution, just omitting the bleach, of course.

You may feel that your working leathers are worthy of distilled or filtered water and, depending on the chemistry of your local tap water, this may be worthwhile. Some tap water is very hard – contains minerals – and may, with sufficient and repeated applications, leave the minerals in the leather. This is probably not a major concern, but a bottle of distilled water costs nearly nothing when compared with the price of a whip or set against the pleasure of a perfectly cleaned instrument.

7) *Treat wooden instruments as you would treat your best wood furniture.* Wooden instruments, like wooden furniture, are made in a variety of ways. Their makers pretty much determine the care you should give them by choosing the finish they are given at the time of manufacture. The best instruments may have

lacquer finishes (these only need mild-soap washing and drying), others are waxed (and should be cleaned and conditioned with high-quality furniture cleaning and conditioning products made for waxed wood). Still other wooden instruments may be produced with a "naked" finish, often a very light wax and sometimes nothing at all. Lightly waxed and "naked" wood will need conditioning to restore moisture as well as cleaning. Any wood with a non-porous finish like lacquer will need no conditioning since the conditioners would not be able to penetrate the wood anyway. The only concern, really, is to see that no product you use in cleaning wood instruments is either leaving a slippery surface or any chemicals that may be dangerous to skin. Pretty obvious, actually. (Note: Take a hint. If you have to wear gloves to apply a product, except to protect your hands from coloration, it is not appropriate to use that product on any SM instrument unless it is to be cleaned away completely as well.)

8) Clean and condition rubber and rubber-like materials with rubber-specific products. Rubber gear and instruments are common enough now that proper products for their maintenance are easily available. Generally, however, the products for cleaning rubber garments are fine on SM instruments; the products made for "conditioning" rubber garments are usually just surface treatments that may be inappropriate for working instruments, depending on how they are to be used. Food-grade sprays and waxes which are commonly used as a final dressing on rubber garments are, of course, safe on SM instruments, but they may make the instruments too slippery to be used safely or conveniently. Cleaning is usually all the maintenance rubber instruments need if they are stored properly.

Storing rubber properly is a matter in which opinions vary surprisingly. Nonetheless, the garment-storing idea of powdering and bagging each item is not usually appropriate for working rubber since you will then have to clean the surface of powder before using the instrument. What we learn from garment storage that does matter very much – and is easy too – is that rubber should not be exposed to (stored in) sunlight.

9) Be sure you know which "other" materials your instruments are made of and how to maintain them. Makers of non-leather, non-rubber, non-wood instruments will almost certainly know how the specific materials they make and use are best cleaned, conditioned and kept. Among the materials are many that may seem to be related to rubber but which, for various reasons, should never be exposed to the cleansers used on rubber. Many of the more commonly used materials in the "other" category are best maintained with no other effort than simple washing, using a grease-cutting dishwashing liquid and warm water. Nitrile, vinyl, higher-density neoprene, Teflon, nylon and many others fall into this category in most applications. If the toy maker can't tell you how to maintain the item, and you must have it, find out what else is made from that material and do the research to discover how that material is maintained by its primary users.

Also, some instrument makers are less than genius in choosing their construction methods. Rarely, you will run into a rubber flogger, for example, that is held together with tacks and has a wood-core handle. While an all-rubber item can be submerged in soapy water for washing, the tacks might rust and the wood might warp. Be watchful for this kind of surprise and work around it, or avoid collecting such hard-to-maintain items.

When you buy an implement made of an unusual material, like this rope cat, ask the manufacturer how to maintain it.

10) Do not over-shampoo your horsehair floggers. While it is not damaging to shampoo horsehair from time to time, it will not last long if it is shampooed every day or every week. Annual shampooing is probably enough if you are taking good care of the horsehair after each use as described below. When you do use shampoo, use a mild one and/or also use a conditioner. Let the horsehair dry completely after washing before you attempt to straighten or brush it. Then, when fully dried, treat the horsehair to it usual after-care.

Regular maintenance for horsehair floggers: After use, the horsehair will probably be clumped together in stringy bunches, it may feel greasy, and it is often also tangled. To correct all these problems in a single operation and get your flogger back in top shape, you will need about 15 minutes per half-inch of hair. (The measurement of horsehair is the diameter of the plug of hair at the point where it is gathered into the handle. Great horsehair floggers are made with everything from 3/8 of an inch to 1 1/4 inches of hair.)

Assuming that you are right-handed, grasp your flogger in your left hand by its hair so that about one or two inches of hair is visible between your hand and the handle of the whip, and the rest of the hair is sticking out the top of your hand. With your right hand, pull no more than two or three hairs at a time from the exposed length between your left hand and the handle. Pull these tiny bundles of hairs until their ends fall from your finger tips. Keep doing this until you have pulled all the hairs – no more than three at a time – out of the grip of your left hand and allowed them to run through the fingertips of your right hand. Have a sturdy plastic hair brush at hand. From time to time, stop and stroke the hairs that have been dropped on your lap or the chair-arm or wherever, just to keep them from becoming tangled after they have been pulled free. When you have freed every hair and your left hand is empty, turn the whip handle-up and brush the hair slowly and thoroughly. Be gentle!

Like human hair, horsehair should be washed and detangled – but too-frequent care can make it limp and fragile.

To store the horsehair flogger, you may want to braid the hair loosely in a simple three-part braid. Alternatively, you could wrap it snugly or just put a rubber band around the loose tips. It is best for a horsehair flogger to be stored hanging by its handle or on a shelf in such a way that the horsehair is hanging off the shelf and is not bent, curved or crimped.

MAINTENANCE OF LEATHER FLOGGERS AND CATS

Flogger and cats need much less care than is often believed. That does not mean they need *no* care. If your flogger or cat has not been used, it probably needs no care, although conditioning may be needed after very long storage, especially if the storage area was not sufficiently humid. (Leather is most "comfortable" in the same range of humidity that humans like best: 35 to 65 percent relative humidity, 50 to 55 percent being optimal.) After use, if there may be blood or stains on the leather of your instruments, follow the instruction given in the general rules above.

For ordinary care, clean as often as you like – once or twice a year, or after 25-30 scenes is probably sufficient, especially if there is no chance of blood on the leather – with the leather cleaner of your choice. Consider saddle soap and follow the directions on the container carefully. Some products may be confusing. They claim to clean *and* condition. This may not be impossible, but it seems unlikely. When you are cleaning, you usually want to remove all residue of the cleaner. When you are conditioning, you want to allow the leather to retain as much of the conditioner as it can actually absorb. It is true that conditioning will loosen soil and foreign materials, allowing them to be wiped away, but it is advisable to clean with a cleaner (like saddle soap) and condition with a conditioner (like dubbin or hard lanolin).

Once the leather is clean, condition it immediately. Cleaning may leave the leather feeling damp, but it actually removes the moisturizing oils from the leather in order to take out the soil and foreign materials. If it leaves behind any dampness, that will evaporate or weep out of the leather. So, reconditioning with a good oil-, wax- or lanolin-based product is vital. Consider Hubberd's Boot Grease and dubbin. Many other products are available and most of them are

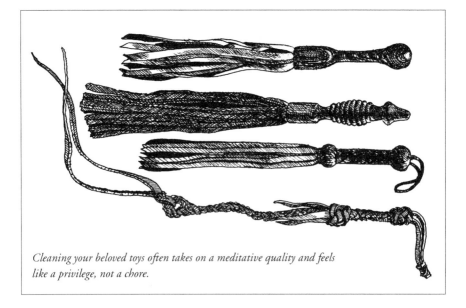

Cleaning your beloved toys often takes on a meditative quality and feels like a privilege, not a chore.

good. You might like to follow the lead and suggestions of a knowledgeable friend who can also oversee and correct your efforts the first time around.

When cleaning braided leather, give the job the extra effort required to work the cleaner into the overlaps of the leather strips and to work the cleaner back out of these traps and crevices. A soft toothbrush may be useful. Then, when conditioning, press hard to work the conditioner into the leather that is hidden from view by the braiding.

When conditioning any leather flogger or cat, but particularly those with flat (unbraided) tails, be sure to especially work the conditioner into the first inch and a half of each tail at the handle end. This is where the leather is most stressed by use, where it dries most completely and where it is will eventually exhaust and break first. Careful conditioning in this area can extend the life of a good leather flogger from a no-care maximum of 5 or 10 years to a careful-conditioning maximum of several decades.

Maintenance of Braided Single-Tailed Whips

The leather and braiding of single-tailed whips need the same kind of treatment and maintenance as that of floggers and cats. What is different with single-tails is that they may well need more conditioning and may need to have it done much more often. And, in fact, it is usually a good idea whenever you condition a single-tail whip to do so several times over a period of days to be sure the conditioner reaches the leather under the braided overlay. Many regular users condition their single-tails before every use. The reason for this is that the fast, cracking action of the whip is much more powerful in forcing moisture out of the leather than the action of floggers and cats. Others worry about over-conditioning because they say it interferes with the "personality" of the whip. This is clearly a matter of personal opinion and, very shortly, you will have your own opinion to work with.

Also, many users say that constant conditioning – several times between uses – of a new single-tail helps it become supple and responsive. This is almost surely true. As you are learning the use and "personality" of a new whip, you may want to keep conditioning it until you have settled on a degree of moisturized weight and suppleness you find optimal. Then you will learn from the whip, by its changes with use, how often and how much work is required to maintain that condition.

Conclusion

Doing What Feels Good

As you become experienced with flogging, you will develop your own style. You will determine for yourself what is and is not safe, what works and does not work. You will discover elements of technique that were not mentioned in this book, and you will – almost certainly – some day find yourself teaching someone else how to handle whips. Whether Top or bottom or, as is so usual these days, switching between Top and bottom, you will be building skills and learning your craft for years to come. Flogging is like that, like any "art," inexhaustible in the possible permutations and the capacity for devlopment.

My personal starting point with flogging did not include any book or instruction, and I'm not sure I would have wanted any. But we live in a different world today. My first flogging experience was a singular event, preceded by no expectations or awareness of any sort, and followed by a desert of no such experience again for a very long time. Now, everyone knows something of SM, often even of flogging. You couldn't watch prime time television for a week or read a major magazine or play video games without running into it in some form. My early partners were unique individuals as far as I knew, rarities, loners. I was shocked to discover that there were more than 20 leathermen in Los Angeles when, in the early '70s, I saw that many in one place for the first time. Of course, there were hundreds or even thousands of leathermen and leatherwomen there even then. I just didn't know them or of them, so I had no idea of how to be in touch with them. And now, major leather events limit their attendance on the basis of how many rooms the host hotel can provide or how many players the dungeon can accommodate. Attendance is often over 1,000, several times a year it is much higher. This is a new world, and mostly a better one – surely, in many ways, a safer one, despite stalking and AIDS and Internet-related "terrors."

If you are new to SM and flogging, you are entering a world in which there is a formula for success: Safe, Sane, Consensual. We say that both to describe to outsiders what SM *is* for us and to remind one another that we do take the trouble to arrange for safety, to discuss our intentions and discover that our partners are appropriate, and to achieve consent or do nothing. You are coming into a world where sex and pain and limits and techniques and relationships are openly and frankly discussed. Take advantage of all the opportunities presented by this openness. Join in the discussions, and become one of the voices heard – even if, for now, you are only heard asking questions.

Far more important, play. Whenever and wherever you get the opportunity to experience flogging – to watch it, to do it, to have it done to you – move to the front of the line and ask if you can join in. To know everything about flogging will do you no good if you don't get out there and test in real life what you have learned.

From the first day, you will have opinions: He is good at this. She has no idea what she is doing. When she does *that* it looks graceful, but when he does *that other thing* it looks out of control. Share your positive opinions of what you see immediately. The effort may get you a friend or it may get you a flogging, or both. Withhold your negative judgments for now. Your opinions may change – especially if you ever get to see yourself in a mirror or on video doing a flogging. Your opinions also will *definitely* change as you get to know the players and techniques you are seeing.

As you watch, you are learning, just as when you read this book, but there is a world of difference between theoretical knowledge from books and observation and practical knowledge from participating. Dive in! Do what feels good for you and, whenever possible, ask your partners to tell you later about their experience playing with you.

If you are a bottom, as you may well be at least in the beginning, it will be useful to know whether your performance included any surprises for the Top or any hard-to-read communications. Perhaps you will want to change or adjust something on the basis of this feedback. Perhaps you will "only" have learned something which, under certain conditions, you will want to communicate to other Tops before they flog you.

If you are a novice Top, don't be afraid to play with experienced bottoms. Take it as your responsibility, however, to tell people you are playing with that you are new to this kind of play. Their feedback can be invaluable, and your mistakes (if any) will not be anything new or frightening to them. And, when you meet a really good Top that you connect with on a personal level, consider taking the bottom role just to further educate yourself about what goes on at that end of the whip.

I treasure my own memories and experience of flogging over the past 36 years, and I prize the skill I have developed, but I still envy newcomers a bit. The wonders you have in store for you are exciting. Allow yourself to feel and explore all of it, and to enjoy it.

I want to leave you with two more ideas to ponder which are best described as the urge to destroy and the impulse of love. They are both integral to my experience of flogging and are, perhaps, far less separate than they sound.

Meeting the beast in myself: When I am doing a flogging and it is going well, there is a very high likelihood that I will eventually find myself "under the influence of" a part of myself I recognize as beastly, a part I have become comfortable thinking of as a lion.

Like any lion, mine loves the smell of blood and wants nothing at all more than it wants to tear its victim apart, shred the body, frolic in ecstatic pleasure in the moment of the "kill," the victory. I could write whole books about this lion-self and his desires, but I believe that it is important to understand this anti-gentle, non-compliant, even violent creature inside. He is vital to keeping SM –

flogging in particular – lively and meaningful for me. Without this urge, the tension for me, as a Top, would be insufficient to make the experience worth repeating.

On the other hand, there must be a force at least equal to and opposing the lion, or we are in real trouble. We do not want the lion running rampant any more than we want this impulse for intensity to be absent. It is all too clear what that means and where it leads. The other side of this balance is love. I never play with anyone at any level beyond a stop-and-go demo without honestly loving them. The love usually lasts longer than the scene, often lingers long enough for us to develop a real and lasting friendship, a loving friendship. This may seem like a big burden to put on your search for partners, but it really isn't. Loving someone, in my understanding, means nothing more than that you want them to have the most and best of everything that is good and useful for them, and being willing to take whatever steps are available to you to see that they get all of that.

So, loving someone enough to play with them only means wanting the most and best of everything that is good and useful for them *right now,* and being willing to play with that in your heart and mind, directing the action of your body. It isn't as much or as hard as it seems, and usually all it means is that you don't let yourself play with someone if you don't feel good about the person – Top or bottom.

Keeping the lion alive and hungry to provide intensity, keeping your heart open and generous to ensure mutuality – you become a Master Flogger – except for the technical practice. So, now, get out there and practice.

Appendix A

Milestones in Modern Whipmaking

by Gayle Rubin

Few people realize how much whips and whipmaking have changed over the last two decades. In the late1970s, there were no established leather craft fairs to facilitate the distribution of work by skilled individuals. In the United States, whips were obtained primarily from leather stores and riding shops. In England, umbrella stores such as Swaine Adeney Brigg also carried canes and riding whips. Uncle Sam's Umbrella Shop in New York was an oddity, and like its British counterparts was a source for flagellation gear.

Most of the whips sold in leather or sex shops were poorly designed and badly made (with a few occasional and notable exceptions). These generally consisted of a few tails cut from inferior leather attached to a wooden handle. A leather cover was glued, tacked, and sometimes taped over the handle. The few commercially available quality whips were usually imported from countries where whipmaking was still a local craft tradition. These were mostly riding crops, but the occasional Mexican quirt, Australian stock whip, or nicely braided cat o' nine tails would appear. Quality single tailed whips were manufactured in this country by David Morgan in Seattle, based on Australian techniques.

In the early eighties, a few craftspeople began to reinvent the SM whip. Some of the best and most influential of these were Robert "Mad Dog" Roberts, Fred Norman, Jim of London, and Jay Marston. Originally, this whipmaking renaissance was a largely west coast phenomenon, and much of it centered in San Francisco.

Robert "Mad Dog" Roberts was one of the first of the new whipmakers. Mad Dog, a multi-talented artist, took up whipmaking around 1982 and quickly produced a few whips that were distinctively designed and markedly superior to anything else in the local shops. Mad Dog made quirts, slappers, soft genital whips, fabulous (if heavy) floggers, blacksnakes, and several types of rubber whips (some of which were fashioned by Robert's partner Tim). These were extremely well crafted and utilized complex traditional braiding techniques. Unfortunately for whip connoisseurs, Mad Dog soon abandoned whipmaking and applied his considerable artistic capabilities to tattooing. He has since become a successful and highly regarded tattoo artist. He left behind some beautiful and durable whips which are treasured by those few enthusiasts lucky enough to have them.

Jim of London was another superb craftsman. He began whipmaking in London in 1984 and continued in San Francisco until he returned to England in 1987. Jim studied and mastered the techniques of both David Morgan, in Seattle, and R.M. Williams, the premier Australian manufacturer of traditional single-tailed herding whips. Jim specialized in finely braided, beautifully constructed single-tailed whips, including blacksnakes, stockwhips, and several kinds of bullwhips. He invented a unique hybrid design which combined elements of quirts and cats o' nine tails. It featured multiple braided tails attached to a short, lead-loaded, single tail-type body. Like Mad Dog, Jim's career was regrettably brief, and he is presently a computer programmer. Both Mad Dog and Jim made wonderful items, but their whipmaking careers too short and their output too scarce for most people to be familiar with their work. As a result, their influence was somewhat limited.

Fred Norman, of Denver, was a skilled hobbyist whose most productive period was also in the mid-eighties, although he still occasionally produces something new even now. His influence can be seen everywhere in today's floggers and color schemes. Fred's early whips were sturdily made, distinctively crafted, and relatively "heavy." A San Francisco friend suggested he try lighter materials, and this resulted in Fred's famous "whisper whips." These whisper whips were made of exquisitely sensual leathers that kissed the skin. Later he experimented by adding ever greater numbers of tails, still in those soft, lovely leathers; he used larger handles to balance the tails. These whips had a unique feel which combined considerable heft with a velvet touch, a strong fist in an exquisitely soft glove. At parties, bottoms would line up to feel their caress.

Fred's whips were balanced and his flogger tails were lush. Fred disliked all-black whips and as a rule refused to make them. His favorite color was red, especially a deep ruby red and a darker oxblood; almost every Fred Norman whip had red in it somewhere, if only on the small piece of round leather capping the handle and embossed with his signature mark. He also pioneered the use of metallic leathers to add glitter to his dazzling braided handles. He often used characteristic slit leather and horizontal handle weaves which have been widely imitated. In addition to floggers, Fred made paddles, straps, and some of the earliest nylon cock and pussy whips. Some of his most sought-after whips had carved wooden handles, many cock-shaped, and all designed to be insertable. While Fred has not entirely abandoned whipmaking, his production has been extremely sparse in recent years.

Perhaps the most influential of the whipmaking innovators was Jay Marston. More than anyone else, Jay established new standards for the SM whip and is largely responsible for today's thriving market in whips. Jay Marston began making whips in 1984, as part of a leather craft business that also included other custom play gear. Demand for her whips rapidly grew until whipmaking became the main, although never the sole, focus of her leather business.

Jay's business, Hedonic Engineering, was well-named: Marston equipment was exquisitely designed, beautifully crafted, and built to enhance sensate experience. She virtually redesigned the floggers and braided multi-tailed whips which were her primary specialty. Jay had been an apprentice to an eminent guitar maker, and she had worked on designs for guitars and other musical equipment. She brought a musician's sensibilities to her whipmaking, approaching whips as sensual instruments. Many people have compared using her whips to playing a fine musical instrument; others credit her with single-handedly expanding the sensory range of whipping experience.

Jay experimented with a great variety of leathers in different weights and densities for floggers and braided cats. When her first whips appeared, most local *cognoscenti* recognized her obvious talent but considered her whips much too big and heavy, as well as awkward to use. This was because her designs were so innovative that few understood how to use them. Most whips then were lighter. They were designed to be gripped in the middle of the handle and were balanced accordingly. Jay's early whips were made with much heavier leathers. She developed new weighting methods which enabled her to change the balance point so that her whips could be swung from their equally innovative finishing knots. Jay introduced large, rounded finishing knots which could roll easily in the hand. With this rolling technique, the weight worked to help power the swing instead of resisting it, and these huge whips were surprisingly easy to use and control. Whips of these sizes, which seemed so radical in 1985, are now commonplace and virtually the standard.

Jay also made braided cats o' nine tails out of leathers of many different weights. This resulted in braided cats which ranged in size from those with thin, sinuous, slicing, speedy tails to cats with thick, heavy, thunderous ones. She was one of the first of the contemporary whipmakers to popularize a traditional flat, no-knot flat tail weave, and she invented the no-knot round braid tails. Jay also expanded the color palette. In addition to basic black, she made whips from red, silver, purple, grey, blue, white, pink, yellow, and green leathers. Initially, the colors were chosen in terms of more traditional SM aesthetics. Red and silver, for example, could also be seen in the piping on uniforms and leather with stylistic features drawn from military and police garb. Purple was a color already associated with piercing. The palette also expanded as individual customers wanted color customization. Some femme dommes began to request pink, watersports enthusiasts yellow, and assorted pagans and faeries desired green to invoke forests and leafy glens.

To the dismay of her devoted clientele, Jay developed severe carpal tunnel injuries from leather braiding, and was retired from active whipmaking by the early 1990s. But her legacy is immense and her influence on the current generation of whipmakers can be seen at every craft fair where the designs and available styles still draw heavily upon her repertoire. Jay's whips were beautifully crafted, and evinced a fantastic attention to detail. Her braiding was extremely tight, the edges were finished, the handles were sealed, and the construction was nearly indestructible in normal use. Because of her creative design innovations and the quality of her craftsmanship, Jay's work has become a standard against which most multi-tailed whips are judged.

In addition, Jay was probably the first of this group of craftsfolk to actually make a living (albeit a physically grueling and financially meager one) as a whipmaker for several years. As a result her output was relatively large and her influence widespread. Her activities helped to create and establish the current market for whips.

Many of the former whipmakers who have left the whip business have done so either because of injury or because it has been extremely difficult to make a decent living from whipmaking. There is a limit on what people seem willing to pay for whips, and some of the best whipmakers, who took more time with their work and used fine but expensive materials, were working for about three to five dollars an hour. Inefficient means of distribution were another serious impediment. The mechanisms for connecting producers with consumers were, by today's standards, rudimentary. While good whipmakers are still not going to get rich, changes in the leather economy currently provide more consistent financial support for leather crafts. There are now several individuals making a full or part time living from whipmaking. This development has been made possible by the luxuriant growth of markets for leather and SM crafts which began to develop in the 1980s.

The emergence of local, regional, and national leather markets was an important phenomenon which, among other things, helped to nurture, distribute, and finance the efflorescence of skilled whipmaking. Such leather markets were beginning to appear by 1980. For example, the Chicago Hellfire Club's renowned Inferno run has long been a focus not only for play but for the dissemination of ideas, techniques, and equipment. The importance of such informal exchanges was recognized and a formalized flea market has been a feature of the run since Inferno X. Another of the earliest leather markets was GMSMA's Bizarre Bazaar, first held in New York in 1981.

It has often been the case in its leather history that San Francisco lagged behind New York and Chicago (as well as Los Angeles), but caught up in spectacular fashion. This was the case with leather markets. In 1984, Lady Thorn founded the Bizarre Flea. This event was later renamed the SM Community Exchange. It celebrated its tenth anniversary in 1994 and is now working on its second decade. The first Folsom Street Fair was also held in 1984. The Bizarre Flea/SM Community Exchange and the Folsom Street Fair have provided regular and consistent sales outlets for Bay Area leather vendors, including local whip producers, ever since. A second South of Market Street Fair (first the Ringold Alley Fair, then the Dore Alley Fair, and generically known as the Up Your Alley Fair) was begun in 1986, although it did not become a sales outlet for leather crafts until the early 1990s. Several other local bazaars and flea markets have emerged in San Francisco as a result of Lady Thorn's success.

Local leather markets have become established in many other areas, including Boston, New York, and Los Angeles. Many of these local fairs also function as regional markets. For example, the Bizarre Flea/SM Community Exchange in San Francisco has grown exponentially, and is predictably held in April, August, and December of every year. The December market now draws vendors from all over the west coast. The Fetish Flea Market in Boston draws customers from all over New England and vendors from even further afield. The markets at regional leather title contests and other leather events similarly draw on and service populations from their surrounding hinterlands.

Since the mid-1980s, there has been a widespread nationalization and even internationalization of such leather markets. The first National Leather Association Living in Leather conference in 1986 had a sales area, as did the SM/Leather Conference at the 1987 March on Washington for Lesbian and Gay Rights. Most regional, national, and international leather events now routinely feature an institutionalized opportunity for the exchange of SM/leather goods. No major event seems complete without a sales fair. Vendor areas and leather markets have become a big part of the action at most of the significant events including Living in Leather, International Mr. Leather, International Mr. Drummer, International Ms. Leather, the SM/Leather Conferences at the Marches on Washington, Black Rose, Stonewall 25, Eulenspiegel 25, Folsom Street East, GMSMA's Leatherfest, The Society of Janus's Twenty Fifth Anniversary, Thunder in the Mountains, Southeast Leatherfest, and MidAtlantic Leather. One of the most extensive markets occurs annually at the now venerable Folsom Street Fair, which has become not only one of the largest leather events in the world but also one of the largest regularly held public events in California, evidently exceeded only by San Francisco Gay Pride and the festivities attending the Rose Bowl.

The characteristics of particular markets at various periods have determined the rate and direction by which information, craft technique, and innovation have penetrated into different geographic areas and demographic groups. For example, the San Francisco markets such as the Bizarre Flea and the Folsom Street Fair have always catered to most segments of the local kinky population. Since gay people, heterosexuals, bisexuals, and transpeople of all genders shop and sell at these events, the circulation of material goods and technologies into different subpopulations has been rapid, if geographically limited.

By contrast, CHC's Inferno market has been international in scope, but has catered exclusively to gay men. However, various CHC members took Jay Marston whips to Inferno, and gay male whipping aficionados enthusiastically adopted them. The buyers there are men, but many of the better goods consistently find their way to Inferno no matter what the gender or sexual orientation of their makers.

Fred Norman's whips had a completely different pattern of distribution, with consequently different results. Fred is based in Denver, but his work sold mainly through friends in New York, San Francisco, and Los Angeles. His whips were snapped up as quickly as litters of prized purebred puppies. They rarely made it to formal sales fairs, and were channeled through networks which were predominantly, although by no means exclusively, heterosexual. His work was best known among kinky heterosexuals in San Francisco, New York, and Los Angeles. While some San Francisco lesbians and gay men were able to buy his work, few gay men or lesbians outside the Bay Area were exposed to it.

The big markets which are now so ubiquitous at national and international events and the major celebrations have overcome many of the structural limitations of place and the boundaries of sexual orientation. Goods and the ideas that animate them now traverse easily from coast to coast, and percolate quickly among all the leather sub-populations. Whipmaking traditions are no longer as locally distinct. But more importantly, the increased size, complexity, and consistency of the leather economy have provided for a level of commercial and craft activity that would have been difficult to envision in 1980.

There are now many distinguished artisans making whips in many parts of the US, and there are numerous opportunities for them to show their wares. This is a dramatic shift from the way things were in the late 1970s. Even the most mediocre of the whips now available are far better than most of what could be obtained then. The best ones would have been unimaginable. We have new kinds of whips which are now widely obtainable, such as the redesigned floggers made popular by western whipmakers and now customarily called "California" or "West Coast" floggers. An even more recent development is a resurgent production and popularity of finely crafted singletailed whips. The abundant and flourishing markets are important mechanisms for sustaining people in the production of kinky arts and crafts.

It is still difficult to make a living as a whipmaker. Many skilled artists have burned out, suffered repetitive stress injuries, or simply gone on to more lucrative forms of employment. If you see a whip you love, buy it now if you can, for you may never see it again. Today's whipmaker will probably be doing something else tomorrow. And do not take the present situation for granted. There was a time, not so long ago, when there were no leather markets, few skilled whipmakers, and a scarcity of quality leather crafts. The economies, technologies, and artistries of play have come a very long way in a very short time, but they could quickly disappear as have the institutional structures of other alternative cultural communities. For example, two decades ago there was a vibrant network of feminist bookstores, coffee houses, and publications. There are some remnants, but this world has mostly vanished. We should cherish what we have, and do what we can to ensure that our tools, technologies, and communities continue to prosper.

Gayle Rubin, San Francisco
© Copyright Gayle Rubin 2000

This article is slightly revised from one appearing in DungeonMaster, number 48, March 1994. Reprinted here by permission of the author.

APPENDIX B

WHERE TO BUY FLOGGERS, WHICH ONES TO BUY

WHIPPING AND FLOGGING ARE NOT FOR everyone, but anyone who likes to flog or be flogged will, sooner or later, have to consider owning a whip. One whip or several. The other thing a person has to consider, often at a later date, is which whips to no longer own, as the collection outgrows the available storage space or the person outgrows the early choices. Both sets of choices – which whip or whips to buy and which whip or whips to dispose of – require some relatively uncommon knowledge.

A very informal survey of a handful of whip owners suggests that the following facts might be true of most people, possibly including yourself. One, most people have and use a very poor whip for some time before they discover what a good whip is. Two, most people get their first whip either as a gift or as a joke.

And, three, most people – even those who use whips frequently – have no idea what to look for if and when they go shopping for a whip. Result A: Most whip collections are composed by accident rather than selection, and they contain good whips and bad in no particular proportion. Result B: Most of the whips owned by most people never get used at all. Instead, they hang on the wall or whip rack "looking good" or, at least, "looking much" while the same one or two whips (out of ten, twenty or more) are used regularly.

CHOOSING A WHIP TO BUY

Obviously, some experience of whips – even if it is experience in fantasy – is called for. You have to have some idea what kind of whip you are (or believe you will be) attracted to. Think about what kinds of visual images and sounds you think are erotic, what kinds of pain or sensation you think of as "real" in connection with whipping. Think about what requirements you have, actual requirements, needs! Think also about what desires you have, and to what extent your desires are important as they relate to the type of whip your might buy.

The same considerations should be applied to your partner if you have a permanent or continuing partner. Or, if you have no partner, consider what you would want your partner(s) to think or feel about the whips you own and use or offer for use on yourself. Suppose, for example, you have worked out what you want: A big-looking whip with a heavy silhouette that makes a loud thud when it hits and leaves bruises more easily than stripes. But, suppose you are a man who prefers to bottom to very petite and feminine women. A big (looking) whip might be pretty heavy for a small woman, but a smaller (shorter) with broader and heavier tails might still give you the thud and bruise you want. If the women who dominate you are unlikely to be able to crash the whip into your tough hide with enough force to give you those much-wanted bruises, you may need to give her a police baton or other rigid instrument for making the bruises *after* the flogging *per se* has tenderized the beaten area.

Such give and take considerations cover all the essentials of whip selection. You want A, and you want it in spades, but A is achieved only with X, a type of instrument that frightens you or your partner. No problem. Think how A-like sensations and results are achieved, and derive a new recipe for getting them.

With whips, you can have any and all sensations, in any and every pattern or order, with any sort of appearance or fantasy you like. It just takes informed care and careful preparation to get what you want.

Here is a list of what you might consider before you go out to buy a whip: Size, fantasy significance if any, color(s), types of material, the recommendations of friends, and personal experience, and probably also available sources. This last point – available sources – improves all the time as more and more leather events have good vendor markets, and increasing numbers of decent whip makers offer their wares on the World Wide Web as well. Hint: Search for flogger on the web. It's that simple to get started.

SIZE

The size of a whip should be considered before you go shopping, mostly in terms of whether a whip of a certain size an be effectively used in the space where you are likely to play. Of course, the size of the whip will vary some depending on your own size or that of your most likely partners. You will want the top to be comfortably able to lift and swing the whip long enough for a complete and satisfying scene. Still, test the size that you think makes sense for you by swinging a piece of rope or some other softly forgiving material in the space where you expect to play. Is there plenty of room, or is there only room enough if you are more careful than you can possibly be in a scene? You don't want to devote a great deal of attention to not whipping a lamp while you are trying to correctly and appropriately strike a bottom.

As to the size of whip for your size of body, one rule of thumb that is "out there" in the marketplace is this: The total length of the whip, from the point at which you will grip it to the portion that makes contact with the bottom, should be no more than two inches longer or shorter than your arm is from the break between arm and shoulder to fingertips. The reason this should work is simple enough to understand. You have lived with your arms all your life. You have developed an automatic understanding of how far away your can reach. Closer, you have to watch carefully. Further away, you have learned to lean or reach. The idea of having the whip match your arm length makes some sense, but it is not the whole story. You'll find other factors that are yours alone that are equally important. This is just a starting point.

FANTASY SIGNIFICANCE

Not every whip evokes fantasy images, nor does every pain-scene fantasy make reference to a whip. Nonetheless, if you are a fantasy player, you will want to consider whether your whips and your fantasies can co-exist. A person who, for instance, fantasizes being brutalized and raped by bad guys, is not likely to find a made-for-SM flogger is much support for the scenario. Floggers made for SM may work well enough when the fantasy is one of punishment – pirates, inquisition, penance, shipboard offenses, bad child, etc. Or, depending on the details you require of the scene, they may not.

Still, if your fantasies are important to you, whatever whips and whipping technique they require may well be worth learning. And, certainly, you will want to own the whip you dream and fantasize about, even if neither you nor your partner is ready to use it right now.

COLOR

Most whips come in black when made for SM and shades of brown when made for just about any other purpose. Lately, other colors have begun to appear. Riding crops and other horse whips are now made in bright red and forest green as well as "international orange" and hot pink. Some of these colors may have purposes. The "fun" colors may help children maintain an interest in riding lessons, for example. And any of them may please you or turn you off.

Meantime, leather/SM community whip makers have done some stunning experiments with color. Purple tanned leather whips on which the edges of the tails are dyed bright blue (by Metz in Australia), "the flame whip," splash dyed in all the colors of fire and autumn (Jeanette Heartwood, now represented by The Toy Bag), black floggers with red and gray braided into the handles (John of Anonymous Leathers, Portland, Oregon). People are having their whips coordinated with their erotic clothing or made in color-matched sets, building up scenes with a theme or accent color. Piercers want purple whips, fisters want red ones, piss fans, yellow, Daddies and boys of all genders and sexes go for deep green, and so on. Everyone has reasons, often ones that reason itself can not explain.

While some players remain hard-core traditionalists – wishing for all toys to be black or dark gray, and accepting colors only when the same instrument is not available in black – color is very much part of the current SM scene. The way to deal with this is to do what *you* want. Choose a color or reject all colors by disregarding them, stick with black (plus bits of gray) or reject all black-dominant traditions by going as colorful as possible. But, whatever you do, do what you have thought about and chosen to do. Otherwise you may eventually decide that your collection is all wrong because of the colors and have to dispose of otherwise excellent whips that happen to be dyed wrong for you.

MATERIALS

Leather comes to mind. That's unavoidable. Most available whips are made of leather, but just saying "leather" doesn't completely answer the question of what materials you want your whips made of. There are many options within and beyond the choice of leather.

First, the non-leather options for whips can be unexpectedly interesting. There are rubber whips and latex ones; most people have seen a few of these and they are widely available. There are whips made of chain (not as severe as they sound in the right hands) and whips made of vinyl. Whips are made of plastics and Teflon, nylon and rope, willow and silicon, wire and vines, cotton braid and just about anything else capable of being cut, extruded or otherwise formed into strips the right size for the purpose. Some of these materials will have fetish value for some people, others will provide better than leather does the exact sensation some people want. Non-leather whips are worth considering, even if many of them are much more expensive, and others much less well made than their leather counterparts.

Second, leather whips don't have to be made of full-grain, or tanned-surface leather from cow hides. Suede of cow hide finds a place in whip making as do many other leathers like deerskin, buffalo, kangaroo, snake, and eel. The skins of legally killed (or found-dead) exotic African animals are sometimes used too. And every leather has its own characteristics, some of them easily discerned, others best investigated with the whip maker who chose the leather.

Leather? OK! Do you want it light or heavy, shiny or dull, oily or dry, sharp-edged or rounded, crisp or soft, dense or marshmallowy? Do you want it braided or just cut into strips? Do you want it in small, narrow bits or in big flat sheets? All kinds of questions ought to be considered and even investigated.

RECOMMENDATIONS AND EXPERIENCE

If friends are recommending a specific whip or whip maker, ask them to be very detailed in telling you why they think you would be interested. If the answer, pushed to its most basic beginning is that the friend hopes to accrue "points" or any kind with the whip maker, ignore the advice. Then look at the product or products in question anyway. Generally speaking, though, friends in your SM network can be trusted can be trusted to tell you what they can reasonably know about whips and whip makers and your likely interest in them. A person whose only SM interest is, say, foot worship, may recommend the whips made by a person with attractive feet rather than one who crafts exceptional whips.

More important than reports from friends, of course, are the reports you have from your own body. *That* felt great, your body tells you, and "that" is a certain cat-o-nine made by, say, Anonymous Leathers for this particular top. So, what to buy? So you buy whips only from Anonymous Leathers? Do you always have this top order you whips for you? Do you simply despair because the "good one" already has an owner who doesn't want to sell it to you? None of that. Get in touch with the whip maker or retailer in question and say, very specifically, "The whip of this description made at this time for this whip user in this city interests and pleases me, I'd like to get one just like that (or different in just this way)."

The more details you can give, the more likely you will quickly arrive at an understanding that leads to owning exactly the whip you want.

AVAILABILITY

It would be nice if everyone could always have every whip he or she wants. It doesn't happen that way. For years, for example, if you wanted one of the justifiably famous whips made by Fred Norman, anyone who owned one would just say "dream on," and that was all you could do. At this writing (2000), Fred Norman is again making some of his whips, but not very many. If you find that the whip of your dreams is one made by one of the other legendary whip makers – Jay Marston, Mad Dog, Jim of London – your only hope is to haunt SM flea markets and leather community "exchanges" until you find what you're looking for. Even then, it probably isn't. Marston whips, especially, are found for sale rather often, but they usually turn out to be shoddy imitations of the work that made Jay so famous. She made works of art in the form of floggers and cats. Look closely.

If the whip maker whose work you learn from experience to admire is still working, act now. Who knew that Norman would retire, that Marston would run into wrist trouble, or that Mad Dog would give up whip making for tattooing? Something like this could happen to any whip maker. Besides, you never know when the lure of earning an actual living or some other tragedy will rob leatherdom of another maker of excellent whips.

Selecting a Whip or Rejecting It

Once you are out shopping, actually looking at whips, there are some specific things to look at. There are details of each whip's construction and action that will help you choose or reject it.

Look at the quality of the material, how it feels and bends, curls around your finger and slides through your hand. Look at how the cut edges of the leather or rubber are done, either smoothly or in sharp angles, in hard, clean cuts or shaggy, sueded fuzziness. Questions of the weight of the material and of the overall whip, the thickness of the material, the suppleness of the material and of the ship itself. Then consider the density of the material. (Given apparently equal quantities of two materials, the denser one will seem heavier despite the fact that it is neither larger nor thicker.) Denser materials, even in lighter weights, can have surprisingly intense impact.

Look at the quality of the craftsmanship. Are the cuts carefully finished? Are the edges even? If you bend a section of a braided tail into an arc approximating a third of a circle, then roll the arc between your fingertips, does it roll evenly, in a smooth, almost invisible motion? Are the knots secure and even? Are the parts of the whip securely joined together? If there is any stitching, first, should there be stitching or is it a cover-up? Then, is the stitching tight and evenly done? Is the dying and edge coloring good? Is the whip balanced as you want it to be?

THE FINAL PRE-PURCHASE TEST

Now, the hard part comes. Swing the whip in mid-air, hitting nothing. If it hangs together enough to seem attractive to you, and the tails also splay apart when expected, keep testing. Strike your own back by swinging the whip around your sides, not over your shoulders. You may also want to strike your own legs. If the surface sensation and the sensations that evolve as the sting settles down are satisfactory, keep testing. Then, if possible, strike the bottom with whom you hope to use the whip. Is your bottom as pleased with the whip as you are?

You want all the tails of the whip to stay more or less together as they fly through the air in a stroke, gathering more snugly together when the speed of the movement is increased, splaying apart somewhat more as you slow down the movement. You want to test the whip at the speed and with the type and style of stroke you use in scenes. The stroke the maker or seller uses may show the whip off to a better advantage, but it may have nothing to do with how the whip will perform for you. Or, perhaps you want to learn that stroke just to be a good steward of an interesting whip.

Do not imagine that every whip maker is wiser or more experienced than you are in the ways of whips. Maybe so, maybe not, and maybe it doesn't matter at all. Trust yourself and your technique instructors, and realize that some people make excellent whips which they don't use at all and don't intend to use ever.

Test whips carefully. Take your time. See that you are allowed to test the whip with your own stroke at your own speed on your own preferred target. Ask your partner and your friends for advice if you like, but don't count on the advice of the salesperson unless you have some good reason to rely on it. Compare similar whips and similar pleasures, and be careful not to buy ten of the same whip from different makers. You'll want to be able to build scenes in a variety of way, so you'll also want to learn to select and use a variety of whips.

THE FINAL FRONTIER

The last consideration when purchasing a new whip has to be the price. If it is the whip you want, and there is any way that you can afford it, price is not an issue. If it is a whip that you could sort of tolerate, but could just as well live without, don't bother buying it. No matter how affordable, a whip you don't use is a pointless expense.

If you wait until you are sure you *must* have a certain whip before you ask the price, you will be thinking to yourself, "Whatever it costs, I have to have it," and the price of $150 or $450 or $1,000 will seem like nothing (even if it means begging the whip maker to set the whip aside for six months while you save up for the purchase).

A good whip is worth a good deal. A great whip is worth a great deal. And a whip you must have is worth any price you must pay to get it, worth any effort you must make to find it, worth everything, including learning to make it yourself if that is what is required.

First published in a slightly different form in <u>Sandmutopia Guardian</u>, issue 12, April 1993, edited by Victoria Baker.

ABOUT THE AUTHOR

JOSEPH W. BEAN, AUTHOR OF *LEATHERSEX:
A Guide for the Curious Outsider and the Serious
Player* and *Leathersex Q & A*, is the Executive
Director of the Leather Archives & Museum.
His work and thoughts can also be found in
Leatherfolk edited by Mark Thompson, *Different Loving* by Brame et al, *SM Classics* edited by
Susan Wright, and *Blue Money* by Carolyn See,
among others. His fiction has been published
in *Happily Ever After* edited by Michael Ford,
Country Rogues and *Rogues of San Francisco* edited by Bill Lee, and in just about every SM-
related gay magazine. He and his slave scott appear in the documentary video *Safe Sane Consensual SM* made by B&D Video, and his widely
published art has been collected in the Brush
Creek Media book *Shadows of Leathersex.* He
has edited books by Guy Baldwin, Jack Rinella,
Mistress Nan and others, and many magazines
including Drummer, Mach, International Leatherman, Powerplay, and Tough Customers, the
latter being one of the half-dozen magazines he
also created.

Mr. Bean was born in Humansville, Missouri, in 1947, and has spent the fifty-plus years since everywhere else, but mostly in San Francisco. He lives alone in Chicago now, collecting laundry and household chores for the slave he will one day have.

ABOUT THE ILLUSTRATOR

Chris M is an artist, writer, dominant, and SM educator active with The Black Rose of Washington DC since 1990. A one-man show of his work was exhibited at the legendary Playhouse Studios of Baltimore, and his work is part of the collection of the Leather Archives and Musuem in Chicago, Illinois.

BIBLIOGRAPHY

BOOKS

The Art of Sensual Female Dominance : A Guide for Women, by Claudia Varrin. Citadel Press, NY.

Beneath the Skins: The New Spirit and Politics of the Kink Community, by Ivo Dominguez, Jr. Daedalus Publishing Company, San Francisco.

Between the Body and the Flesh: Performing Sadomasochism, by Lynda Hart. Columbia University Press, New York.

The Bottoming Book: Or, How To Get Terrible Things Done To You By Wonderful People, by Dossie Easton & Catherine A. Liszt. Greenery Press, Emeryville, CA.

Come Hither: A Commonsense Guide to Kinky Sex, by Gloria Brame, Ph.D. Fireside Books, NY.

Coming to Power: Writings and Graphics on Lesbian S/M, by Samois. Alyson Publications, Boston.

Consensual Sadomasochism: How to Talk About It and How to Do It Safely, by William A. Henkin, Ph.D. and Sybil Holiday. Daedalus Publishing Co., San Francisco.

Different Loving: The World of Sexual Dominance and Submission, by Gloria G. Brame, William D. Brame, and Jon Jacobs. Random House, NY.

Erotic Power: An Exploration of Dominance and Submission, by Gini Graham Scott. Carol Publishing Group, New York.

Jay Wiseman's Erotic Bondage Handbook, by Jay Wiseman. Greenery Press, Emeryville, CA.

Learning the Ropes: A Basic Guide to Safe and Fun S-M Lovemaking by Race Bannon. Daedalus Publishing Company, San Francisco.

Leatherfolk, edited by Mark Thompson. Alyson Publications, San Francisco.

Leathermen Speak Out: An Anthology on Leathersex by Jack Ricardo. Leyland Publications, NY.

Leathersex: A Guide for the Curious Outsider and the Serious Player, by Joseph Bean. Daedalus Publishing Co., San Francisco.

Leathersex Q&A: Questions about Leathersex and the Leather Lifestyle Answered by Joseph W. Bean, by Joseph Bean. Daedalus Publishing Co., San Francisco.

The Leatherman's Handbook, by Larry Townsend. LT Publications, Los Angeles.

The Lesbian S/M Safety Manual, edited by Pat Califia. Alyson Publications, Boston.

The Loving Dominant, by John Warren. Greenery Press, Emeryville, CA.

The Master's Manual: A Handbook of Erotic Dominance, by Jack Rinella. Daedalus Publishing, San Francisco.

The Mistress Manual: A Good Girl's Guide to Female Dominance, by Mistress Lorelei. Greenery Press, Emeryville.

My Private Life: Real Experiences of a Dominant Woman, by Mistress Nan. Daedalus Publishing Company, San Francisco.

On the Safe Edge: A Manual for S/M Play, by Trevor Jaques. WholeSM Publishing, Toronto.

Pain and Passion: A Psychoanalyst Explores the World of S&M, by Robert J. Stoller. Plenum Publishing Corporation, NY.

Safe, Sane, Consensual – And Fun, by John Warren. Diversified Services, Boston.

Screw the Roses, Send Me the Thorns, by Philip Miller & Molly Devon. Mystic Rose Books, Fairfield, CT.

Sensuous Magic A Guide for Adventurous Lovers, by Pat Califia. Masquerade Books, NY.

Sex Tips from a Dominatrix, by Patricia Payne. Regan Books, NY.

SM Classics, ed. Susan Wrigh, Masquerade Books, New York.

SM 101: A Realistic Introduction, by Jay Wiseman. Greenery Press, Emeryville, CA.

S&M: Studies in Dominance and Submission, by Thomas S. Weinberg. Prometheus Books, New York.

Ties That Bind: The SM/Leather/Fetish Erotic Style – Issues, Commentaries and Advice, by Guy Baldwin. Daedalus Publishing, San Francisco.

Urban Aboriginals, Geoff Mains, Leyland Publications, San Francisco.

BDSM/KINK

The Artisan's Book of Fetishcraft *(fall 2013)*
John Huxley $27.95

At Her Feet: Powering Your Femdom Relationship
TammyJo Eckhart and Fox $14.95

... But I Know What You Want: 25 Sex Tales for the Different
James Williams $13.95

The Compleat Spanker
Lady Green $12.95

Conquer Me: girl-to-girl wisdom about fulfilling your submissive desires
Kacie Cunningham $13.95

Erotic Tickling
Michael Moran $13.95

Family Jewels: A Guide to Male Genital Play and Torment
Hardy Haberman $12.95

The Human Pony: A Guide for Owners, Trainers and Admirers
Rebecca Wilcox $27.95

Intimate Invasions: The Ins and Outs of Erotic Enema Play
M.R. Strict $13.95

Jay Wiseman's Erotic Bondage Handbook
Jay Wiseman $16.95

The Kinky Girl's Guide to Dating
Luna Grey $16.95

The (New and Improved) Loving Dominant
John Warren $16.95

The Mistress Manual: A Good Girl's Guide to Female Dominance
Mistress Lorelei $16.95

The New Bottoming Book
The New Topping Book
Dossie Easton & Janet W. Hardy $14.95 ea.

Play Piercing
Deborah Addington $13.95

Radical Ecstasy: SM Journeys to Transcendence
Dossie Easton & Janet W. Hardy $16.95

The Seductive Art of Japanese Bondage
Midori, photographs by Craig Morey $27.95

The Sexually Dominant Woman: A Workbook for Nervous Beginners
Lady Green $11.95

SM 101 A Realistic Introduction
Jay Wiseman $24.95

GENERAL SEXUALITY

A Hand In the Bush: The Fine Art of Vaginal Fisting
Deborah Addington $13.95

The Jealousy Workbook: Exercises and Insights for Managing Open Relationships *(fall 2013)*
Kathy Labriola $19.95

Love In Abundance: A Counselor's Advice on Open Relationships
Kathy Labriola $15.95

Phone Sex: Oral Skills and Aural Thrills
Miranda Austin $15.95

Sex Disasters... And How to Survive Them
C. Moser, Ph.D., M.D. & Janet W. Hardy $16.95

Tricks... To Please a Man
Tricks... To Please a Woman
both by Jay Wiseman $13.95 ea.

When Someone You Love Is Kinky
Dossie Easton & Catherine A. Liszt $15.95

TOYBAG GUIDES:
A Workshop In A Book $9.95 each

Age Play, by Bridgett "Lee" Harrington

Basic Rope Bondage, by Jay Wiseman

Canes and Caning, by Janet W. Hardy

Chastity Play, by Miss Simone *(spring 2014)*

Clips and Clamps, by Jack Rinella

Dungeon Emergencies & Supplies, by Jay Wiseman

Erotic Knifeplay, by Miranda Austin & Sam Atwood

Foot and Shoe Worship, by Midori

High-Tech Toys, by John Warren

Hot Wax and Temperature Play, by Spectrum

Medical Play, by Tempest

Playing With Taboo, by Mollena Williams

Greenery Press books are available from your favorite on-line or brick-and-mortar bookstore or erotic boutique, or direct from The Stockroom, www.stockroom.com, 1-800-755-TOYS.
These and other Greenery Press books are also available in ebook format from all major ebook retailers.